I0128100

CAUGHT *in the* CROSSHAIRS

Comedy & Culture

Nick Marx and Matt Sienkiewicz, series editors

CAUGHT *in the* CROSSHAIRS

Feminist Comedians and the Culture Wars

Amber Day

Indiana University Press

This book is a publication of

Indiana University Press
Herman B Wells Library 350
1320 East 10th Street
Bloomington, Indiana 47405 USA

iupress.org

© 2025 by Amber Day

All rights reserved

No part of this book may be reproduced or utilized in any form
or by any means, electronic or mechanical, including photocopying
and recording, or by any information storage and retrieval system,
without permission in writing from the publisher.

First printing 2025

Cataloging information is available from the Library of Congress.

ISBN 978-0-253-07314-3 (hdbk.)
ISBN 978-0-253-07315-0 (pbk.)
ISBN 978-0-253-07316-7 (web PDF)
ISBN 978-0-253-07317-4 (ebook)

For Lira Day McEvoy

CONTENTS

ACKNOWLEDGMENTS

This book was written in snatches across a longer period than I had originally hoped. As such, it went through a number of stages, with an array of folks lending support or consenting to read pieces of it.

Among its first backers was the Johannesburg Institute for Advanced Study, which granted me a writing fellowship in the ill-fated spring of 2020. Though I had to leave the residency early due to the pandemic, the weeks that I did have were very helpful for building out the conceptual structure of this book, and I am grateful for them. I also appreciated the camaraderie and encouragement of all of the other fellows.

Thanks to both Jared Champion and Matt Sienkiewicz who both heroically read through very early drafts and helped me figure out where I was going. Thanks also to Jen Horan, Nick Marx, and Stephanie Carter, who reviewed particular chapters and provided timely advice. Likewise, the input of the Indiana University Press readers was incredibly helpful in shaping the project.

I am additionally appreciative of the time with my "frolleague" Viveca Greene. Besides her fun companionship, the piece we wrote together some years back provided the foundation for some of the ideas I developed further in the Amy Schumer chapter.

Most importantly, I must thank my patient and supportive little family—Patrick, Auden, and Lira—who provide the best distractions and who are all entirely OK with my random outbursts of animal noises and ridiculous accents. This book is dedicated to Lira; funny and fierce, she will surely be transgressing boundaries of her own soon enough.

CAUGHT *in the* CROSSHAIRS

1

Ambivalence

Feminist Comedy Past and Present

IN RECENT YEARS, a greater number of female comedians have been reaching large audiences. Fueled by microtargeting industry trends across much of the globe that encourage producers to take a chance on more "niche" projects and edgier material, we are seeing more female performers in high-profile roles: as late-night hosts, sketch comedians, television producers, and stand-up comedy stars. These comedians have been speaking forthrightly about issues that concern them, introducing new topics and new frames with which to process old topics while often drawing attention to structural inequalities. This means that there has been an upsurge in undisguised feminist comedy. As such, many female and feminist-identified performers have also become the object of a seething backlash, targeted for online attack by the alt-right and "men's rights" groups and sneered at in the conservative press. After the first election of Donald Trump in the United States, and the authoritarian turn more widely, the reactions to outspoken female performers seem to have become even more polarized. In addition to targeted trolling, many female comedians have also attracted generalized controversy, becoming the momentary object of cultural fascination or outrage. In recent years, there have been a great many public discussions and moments of cultural self-reflection as well as of amazement, anger, controversy, and hope that have revolved around feminist comedians.

This book is to some degree about the work of particular contemporary feminist comics such as Samantha Bee, Amy Schumer, Leslie Jones, Michelle Wolf, and Hannah Gadsby, but it is even more so about the discourse around their work. Public discussions about these performers—in the press, online forums, and social media spats—have at times become enormously impassioned. It is my contention that the rhetorical combat is frequently over much larger philosophical and political issues, such as what it means to be a woman or the nature of power and privilege. Ultimately, this book positions feminist comedy as a hot spot in the "culture wars," a site of battle over cultural conceptualizations of gender, race, power, and public space.

I should note that the performers profiled here were not chosen because they are objectively the best female comedians of the day, the most political, or even my personal favorites. Neither have these women somehow nominated themselves as objects of study, nor have they laid claim to exemplary status. Rather, the culture has itself chosen them by momentarily concentrating emotions around their work. Each has attracted an unanticipated flood of attention around a particular routine, movie, or series of work, finding themselves the fleeting objects of mass fascination and critique. Leslie Jones, for instance, became the target of one of the first publicly noticeable, coordinated trolling attacks simply by being part of the cast of a female-centered *Ghostbusters* remake. While the movie was the original object of attack, as the lone Black woman in the principal cast, Jones became the recipient of a fire hose of racist and sexist vitriol. For her part, Amy Schumer began her career to accolades for successfully appealing to both feminists and bros but very quickly became the object of loathing from factions on both the political right and the left, serving as something of a straw woman for all the perceived ills of white feminism. Michelle Wolf and Samantha Bee both were momentary targets of cultural controversy in the spring of 2018 when segments from each of their comedy routines went viral for their perceived rudeness and offensiveness, which elicited impassioned hot takes from commentators of all stripes. Finally, Hannah Gadsby's Netflix special *Nanette*, which challenged audiences by confronting them with difficult material and by subverting expectations around the stand-up genre, garnered an incredible amount of cultural debate. While there was some trolling, there was also an outpouring of support from commentators who latched on to the special as a cultural node of identification. Though not necessarily by design, all of these performers ended up at the eye of a societal storm as various factions grappled to control the narrative around them and to stake out their own visions of appropriate behavior for women in the public sphere. These often-contentious cultural conversations repeatedly shadow feminist comedians in particular.

While I describe my focus as "feminist" comedians, I am deliberately a little squishy on what that category includes. I acknowledge that, as Joanne Gilbert argues, "the genres of 'female' and 'feminist' stand-up comedy, often conflated and frequently assumed without clear definition or delineation" (170), can be problematic. There is hardly a clear benchmark in place with which to measure just how feminist a comic is. And of course, even the most ardently feminist of performers does not focus every single one of their jokes on gender inequality; likely it's not even the majority of their material. Ultimately, however, I believe that the label "feminist" comedian is an important one in these cases, because the performers included in this book are viewed as feminists by both fans and (especially) foes. While most of them (if not all) also do identify as feminist, the focus of the volume is very much on the discourse around each of them, often discourse that they themselves cannot control. As Amanda Philips explains, "one does not actually have to be a feminist to experience the force of rage that is born from antifeminism" (31). Importantly, they are also all female. There are certainly male feminist comics out there as well as those who are trans or nonbinary. While the male feminist comics may receive their share of ridicule from antifans, they do not attract the same level of outrage, revulsion, and general scrutiny. They do not tend to inspire the same number of comedic controversies or spark quite as much cultural debate. On the other hand, those who identify as nonbinary are still so marginal in popular culture that they face enormous barriers to mainstream professional success. Likely for that reason, at the time of writing, there are no nonbinary comedians with quite a high enough profile to spark the sort of widespread cultural conversation chronicled in this volume (though I will touch on the current culture wars over trans individuals in the conclusion). So, more specifically than simply feminist comedians, this book focuses on female-identified, feminist comedians— whose embodiedness is central to the way in which they are received, and often to the material they create.

Of course, the type of feminism that each of these comedians espouses varies a fair amount. Since the invention of the word *feminism*, there has been no stable consensus on what it actually means, beyond a broad focus on women's rights and well-being. In contemporary popular culture, for instance, figures as disparate as Megyn Kelly, Chappell Roan, and Samantha Bee are all framed as feminists (by different constituencies). T-shirts sold at Walmart proudly proclaim "Girl Power," while abortion loses its protection as a constitutional right in the United States. Indeed, that reality of flux and contention is central to the focus of this book. *Feminism* is a spongy term that is filled in by different constituencies in different ways, repeatedly claimed and reclaimed, co-opted by opponents who are arguably hostile to many of feminism's aims, or reimagined in a manner that is advantageous to capital, as in the largely "postfeminist" consumer culture that surrounds us (see Gill; Spigel and McRobbie). It is a term that is always under contestation. For that reason, I will refrain from offering my own definition but will instead trace the ways in which it is leveraged in discussions around these comedians.

As this book contends, feminist comedy is a hot spot in the wider culture wars, the ongoing public contestations around cultural values, priorities, and moral boundaries. Of course, the term *culture wars* is another somewhat squishy one. Stephen Prothero describes culture wars (in the American context) as "battles over symbolic worlds," explaining that "through culture wars, from Jefferson to Obama and beyond, Americans have defined and redefined themselves" (3). The term was not widely used until the 1990s, though Prothero makes the argument that the United States has been riven by culture wars since its inception (7). Since the term has become part of our discourse, it has been used in a variety of ways. Some political partisans have proudly applied the term to their own actions, making the case to the public that they are personally going to war over a social issue or issues that they believe to be of crucial importance to the nation's morality. For instance, the Fox News pundit Bill O'Reilly titled his 2006 book *Culture Warrior*. In it, he argues that the United States is in the midst of a war between the traditionalists (such as himself) and the secular-progressives, who, he implies, are sneakily effecting massive change through domination of the media and the judiciary. Others (particularly on the left) have used the term disparagingly, as a descriptor of a political opponent's cynical attempt to gin up outrage over a nonissue. In some senses then, the term is itself a site of contestation, a concept filled in somewhat differently in different contexts by different actors. Whether spun with a positive or negative valence, though, what remains stable is that culture wars are over values and belief systems. Importantly, they also frequently take place around the work and public personas of women and racial and sexual minorities.

One of the first, very public, so-named culture war battles in the United States took place in and around the congressional hearings over the "NEA

Four" that occurred in the early 1990s. Four different performance artists—Karen Finley, Tim Miller, John Fleck, and Holly Hughes—were initially approved for National Endowment for the Arts (NEA) grants by the regular peer review process. However, under pressure from the religious Right, Congress amended the organization's regulations, stipulating that it could not grant awards based solely on artistic merit but must also consider "general standards of decency and respect for the diverse beliefs and values of the American public" (Halperin C6). The four artists subsequently had their grants rescinded, but they banded together to sue the NEA, leading to public hearings and salacious coverage of the "obscene" content of their art. It is not a coincidence that three of the four artists publicly identified as gay, while the fourth, Karen Finley, referenced the AIDS crisis in her work as well as sexual violence and the objectification of women. Finley, who, of the four, largely became the public face of the case, was famously pilloried by Congressman Jesse Helms, who referred to her as "a nude, chocolate smeared woman" (Finley) since her piece about the violation of women's bodies involved spreading chocolate frosting on her bare torso.

There are a number of through lines from this controversy to those of the present-day comedians examined in this book. These artists attracted widespread cultural condemnation, often from people who had never actually seen their work but who were certain that it was irredeemably obscene and offensive, largely inflected by the performers' difference (as women and sexual minorities) and what were deemed acceptable or unacceptable ways for them to express themselves. I would argue that the very idea of their art was perceived as a threat to male identity and traditional gendered norms. While that was not the only narrative expressed in public, it was most definitely the dominant narrative. (In the contemporary examples, there are often more clearly a number of competing narratives vying for supremacy.) As a result of the notoriety, like many of the comedians of this volume, they were subjected to harassing phone calls, death threats, and what Hughes referred to as "a campaign of public humiliation" (Harris). Where the cases diverge is that the NEA Four, prior to the controversy, worked in the relatively obscure realm of performance art, a corner of the art world that is not normally considered all that important or accessible by the majority of the country were it not subject to congressional scrutiny (indeed, the perceived marginality of their work was also sneeringly used against them). The case studies profiled in this book take place more firmly within the realm of popular culture, as the comedy industry is one that feels familiar for many. Further, social media has now ensured that these sorts of controversies can become the simultaneous subject of conversation for millions of people at once, heightening the speed and intensity of public reaction.

Though there is a tendency to dismiss the products of popular culture as "just entertainment" and therefore peripheral to the more serious forms of political debate, this short-sighted assumption ignores the fact that it is through the more accessible, widely shared world of popular culture that we absorb the majority of our beliefs, ideologies, and cultural narratives. As Stuart Hall explains, popular culture "is the arena of consent and resistance. It is partly where hegemony arises, and where it is secured" (192). While there is inevitably a dominant cultural discourse, one that typically aligns with the interests of the dominant groups, societies are always multidiscursive, with divergent worldviews and assumptions pushing against each other at any given time. Within entertainment media, this is happening at the level of plot, narrative framing, casting, and so on, each thick with layers of discursive contestation. This is true of many media forms (including television dramas, blockbuster films, best-selling novels, and reality television), but it can become particularly visible when a genre is in flux or is facing a challenge from previously marginalized populations. As more and more women and minorities are pushing their way into the business of comedy, they are disturbing old paradigms. The stakes are high for feminist comedy, which has become a microcosm of the political battleground writ large. In and around the work of these comedians, we see contestations over what should be considered scandalous or beyond the pale, who should be in the intended audience, what is appropriate behavior for which performing bodies, and what the boundaries of comedy ultimately are. As such, it is a particularly rich site of inquiry, with the potential to tell us much about our moment.

Comedy and the Work of Politics

Of all art forms, those that involve comedy are the ones most consistently dismissed as being of little consequence. Since the comedic is often simplistically thought of as the opposite of seriousness, the related assumption tends to be that comedic expressions are simply not all that consequential. But that logic does not hold up under scrutiny. As comedy scholars have demonstrated, all humor challenges norms on some level—ranging from scientific norms (like the laws of physics) to social norms (like the prohibition against public

flatulence or the reverence granted to authority). We laugh when our expectations are upended in a comic bit, when the norms we have come to expect are
disobeyed in some way. Thus "all humor carries the potential for reflection on,
or even criticism of those norms" (Gray et al. 9). Theorists think about this
in different ways. In Sigmund Freud's view, tendentious jokes provide a way
for us to let out unconscious desires and repressed feelings, particularly our
stirrings of aggression against the institutions and people who make us feel
powerless. Perhaps the most consequential of theorists on comedy and power
is Mikhail Bakhtin, who argued that laughter allows us to approach an object
or institution from a distanced vantage point, holding it up for examination
(similar to Bertolt Brecht's ultimate goal of "alienation" in political art, which
asks us to consider what we otherwise take for granted in a new light).

Bakhtin's most enduring concept is his theory of carnival. He focuses on
medieval-era carnival, special festival times when the highly regulated medieval society was temporarily turned upside down, when social hierarchies,
norms, and restrictions were briefly lifted, and people acted in ways that
would be unacceptable during the rest of the year. He coined the term *carnivalesque* to refer to the cluster of characteristics that were on display during
these carnivals. One of these was hierarchy inversions. As Bakhtin explains,
during carnival, fools were crowned kings and kings mocked as fools, allowing relief from rigid social structures. Another defining characteristic is what
he terms "grotesque realism," which emphasizes and exaggerates images of
bodies, particularly those engaged in the processes of eating, defecating, and
copulating. It both universalizes and celebrates our gross embodiedness while
ensuring that we don't take ourselves too seriously, reveling in degradation
and the "lowering of all that is high, spiritual, ideal, abstract" (19–20). While
he explains that all are implicated in this type of humor, as it brings us all
down to the same level, it is important to remember that some have further
to fall than others. Accordingly, Bakhtin sees these temporary eruptions of
popular energy as a form of resistance to power, a way of subversively pushing
against social norms and envisioning alternatives. His theory has been taken
up and used as an example of the battle between popular cultural energies
and the forces of authority that try to contain them, so it is a way of reading
popular culture, and comedy in particular, as potentially subversive—a place
where social authority and social norms can be playfully challenged.

Of course, Bakhtin has also been critiqued for being overly optimistic
about the power of carnival. Susan Purdie, for instance, argues that carnival

times were licensed affairs, scheduled releases of steam that kept the peasants content enough to avoid real rebellion. But others have countered that real revolutions often did take place directly after carnival periods, likely because it encourages imaginings of alternatives. Regardless, one of Bakhtin's blind spots is his lack of consideration to the possibility that the carnivalesque can also be used to demonize weaker, not just stronger, social groups. I think it is important to remember that the power of carnival is not the exclusive property of those in possession of progressive political goals (as we will see, President Trump has remained adept at using the carnivalesque mode in the service of deeply conservative or reactionary aims). No matter its political overtones, however, I would argue that the concept helps describe the texture of a lot of contemporary comedy that encourages release from social restrictions and flirts with the subversion of taken-for-granted power structures, social restrictions, and dominant norms.

In much of my previous work, I have labored to demonstrate that satire and irony in particular help advance political dialogue and frequently shift the cultural conversation. That has involved countering two predominant cultural assumptions. The first is an offshoot of the previously described tendency to dismiss comedy as inconsequential. More specifically, it is the idea that the use of irony is inevitably fueled by smirking cynicism and, by extension, political disengagement. It is this assumption that drove all of the premature announcements that in the wake of the 9/11 terrorist attacks, irony would henceforth be dead, presumably because smart alecks everywhere would have to wise up and take things seriously now that we were living in a more obviously dangerous world. In actuality, the attacks, and the attendant rush to war without adequate scrutiny of our motives and tactics, ushered in a golden age of irony. However, during the renaissance of irony and satire that followed, those same suspicions about irony were what fueled numerous articles written about Jon Stewart and *The Daily Show* that warned that he was teaching his fans to be cynical about politics, which would inevitably cause folks to stop caring about the political. As I and many others have demonstrated, however, *The Daily Show* and its many progenies often spend more time fleshing out the background and the stakes of the political issues of the moment than do straight news programs. They also draw attention to the ways in which both politicians and the press work to cloud political discussion, and they urge the development of solutions. In other words, they overwhelmingly encourage political engagement rather than disengagement.

This brings us to the second assumption that must be dispelled. When *The Daily Show* and *The Colbert Report* were at the height of their popularity in the aughts, journalists frequently tried to measure the "effect" of these shows by posing the question, Would they have a demonstrable impact on whatever election was closest? Those who wish to measure satire's efficacy this way, as a one-to-one relationship between consumption and political action, nearly always conclude that satire does not have any real effect in the end. But this is an almost impossibly high bar to meet for any form of art or culture, as humans are not so malleable that we can be instantly swayed by a single text. As I have argued elsewhere, it also reduces all democratic politics down to what one does at the polls, ignoring all of civic life outside of and leading up to the infrequent moments when we vote. Rather, I would suggest that more useful measurements would be a text's ability to excite and galvanize audience members or to influence wider social and political discourse. Satire, one of the most obviously politicized forms of comedy, is particularly good at providing new frames with which to process existing issues, introducing new terms to the discussion, puncturing the authority of those dominating debate, creating a sense of community among those who appreciate the critique, and ultimately shifting the direction of public conversation. Much of this work is gradual but perceptible nonetheless.

In other words, comedy, often derided as frivolous, apolitical, or cynical, "is able to deal powerfully with serious issues of power and politics" (Gray et al. 11). That is not to say that all comedy is equally political or impactful. That is clearly not the case. How it functions socially and politically relies on a shifting combination of authorial intention, craft, audience reception, and social context. But we can say that, across the board, whether in the realm of parodic news, stand-up comedy, or viral video, comedy tends to be at its most powerful and potent when it transgresses norms. Bakhtin's theory of the carnivalesque is so foundational in comedy studies precisely because it does such a good job of describing this element—the pleasurable frisson that comes from witnessing a prohibition ignored or a social structure turned on its head. But transgression is always risky business. If one's transgressions are seen to have gone "too far," one is just as likely to attract a torrent of condemnation. As we will explore, women in comedy are, in many ways, already transgressing cultural norms and expectations the moment they step onto a stage. It is for this reason that female comedians elicit such powerful emotions from audience members, from admiration to disgust, anger, and resentment.

Women and Comedy

There is a lengthy history of seeing women as constitutionally unfunny, a belief that is intertwined with broader assumptions about "natural" gender roles and who belongs in what kind of space. As Linda Mizejewski points out, there has long been an implicit binary set up for women that pits "pretty" and "funny" in opposition to one another (1). Rooted in the history of treating women as property to be traded by men is the belief that a woman's worth is largely defined by her beauty. If heterosexual desirability is a woman's ultimate goal, it is only the otherwise unattractive women who would cultivate the traditionally male attribute of being funny, meaning that their femininity is itself suspect. Indeed, journalist and cultural commentator Christopher Hitchens published an essay in 2007 dedicated to the continued endorsement of this line of thinking titled "Why Women Aren't Funny," wherein he expounded on the supposed biological basis for women's lack of humor, wildly distorting the scientific studies he used to make his point (Krefting, *All Joking Aside* 106). As Linda Mizejewski and Victoria Sturtevant explain, because "the edginess of comedy is understood to be something unnatural to women" (2), a woman's unruly comic transgressions are pathologized in a way that men's typically are not, working against women's participation in comedy.

One way that some female comics have historically managed to sidestep the suspicion and unease directed at funny women has been to practice self-deprecation, making themselves the butt of the jokes rather than a source of power or authority, thereby signaling that they are not a threat and ingratiating themselves with audiences. Frequently this self-deprecation has taken the form of playing into the performer's inability to live up to ideals of female beauty and behavior, arguably reinforcing the pretty/funny binary. Eleanor Tomsett argues that, in many ways, women's self-deprecatory humor simultaneously both conforms to and challenges stereotypical attitudes toward women. As she explains, "women's experiences continue to be marginalised and side-lined in wider society and so in comedy an exploration of how the pressures of body orthodoxy, the failure to conform to body norms or gender stereotypes through selfdeprecation can be read as acknowledgement and validation that these issues and feelings of inadequacy exist" ("Positives and Negatives" 4). Nevertheless, as I will explore in chapter 5, one of the most widely celebrated aspects of Hannah Gadsby's comedy special *Nanette* is Gadsby's explicit rejection of self-deprecatory humor, which they argue serves only to further diminish those who are already marginalized. Though it was not without contention, it was a statement that was tailored to its moment in 2018, when audiences were newly receptive to that sort of critique, but likely would not have been legible previous to that moment. Indeed, Gadsby's self-presentation as a gender nonconforming butch lesbian, a subject position that is still threatening to many, is one that was entirely absent from mainstream comedy until very recently.

If funny women are seen as suspect (or assumed to be nonexistent), the very idea of a funny feminist woman has long been seen as such a contradiction in terms as to be a punchline in itself. As Taylor Nygaard explains of images of feminism in popular culture, "feminists have been caricatured as old, aggressive, anti-sex, man-hating, ugly, and above all humorless" (64). The fact that feminists have insisted on drawing attention to gendered violence, inequality, and messy reproductive issues despite mainstream discomfort has allowed them to be broadly stereotyped as "killjoys" (Ahmed 50–87) who seek to take away anything that others might find fun. The passion that drives individual activists is recast as irrational anger that is supposedly in opposition to humor, enjoyment, or likability. Indeed, there is a ready label that sums it all up; according to Barbara Tomlinson, "angry feminist" is a trope that is "designed to delegitimize feminist argument even before the argument begins, to undermine feminist politics by making its costs personal, and to foreclose feminist futures by making feminism seem repulsive to young women" (1). Or as Phillips puts it, invoking the specter of the angry feminist is designed "to kick actual feminists out of a conversation in favor of a cultural construction that stands in for the absurdity [and] irrationality of feminist critique" (64). Thus, the popular understanding of feminism is one that is always already tinged with associations of excessive anger, self-seriousness, irrationality, and lack of humor.

All of the aforementioned is, importantly, both a way of stigmatizing particular forms of femininity as undesirable and a refusal to hear about women's concerns. Mizejewski and Sturtevant observe that there are political implications to the myth that women are less funny, as "it discourages women from making use of wit and satire to point out injustices and often marginalizes them when they do" (4). In other words, the myth is a self-perpetuating barrier to women using comedy as a means of expression. Sometimes this deep-seated cultural bias simply makes women's issues illegible to male audience members and gatekeepers. In the world of literary satire, for example, "women writers have often used irony to expose abuses of patriarchal power and authority, but their satire was often missed—or misunderstood—precisely because the ironic context of their attack went unnoticed by male readers or critics" (Coletta 209). In such cases, women are rendered, once again, simply not funny. In other cases, women's comedy is perhaps legible as comedy but is assumed to be of niche appeal and is ghettoized as its own arcane subcategory of comedy that couldn't possibly speak to a wide audience. Even as some of the economic incentives for limiting the opportunities of female comics are changing, as niche-focused media becomes its own market strategy, these cultural biases still hold strong. In an article about comedian Amy Schumer, Shaina Hammerman elucidates why the Jewishness of male comedians is often read as more salient than it is for female comedians like Schumer. She points out that because men's comedy is seen as for everyone and women's comedy as just for women, "Jewish men are marked as Jewish. Jewish women are marked first as women and only secondarily, parenthetically as Jewish" (62). As Tomsett puts it, "the right to be considered a comedian (rather than a female-comedian) is central to current debates around women and comedy" ("Twenty-first Century Fumerist" 2). It is near impossible for any individual female performer to fully escape the historical baggage around women and comedy.

That is not to say, however, that the experience of every female comic is the same. On the contrary, all the intersectional elements of a performer's identity impact her reception on stage, including race, sexuality, class, disability status, and so on. As I explore in the next chapter, for instance, the horrific harassment Leslie Jones suffered in the rollout of the *Ghostbusters* movie was aimed very specifically at her identity as a Black woman, a phenomenon referred to by Moya Bailey as "misogynoir," a particularly targeted combination of racism and sexism influenced by historical representations of Black womanhood. Women of color have almost universally faced even more barriers to success in comedy than white women.

Nevertheless, despite the considerable cultural and structural roadblocks for women in comedy, there have, of course, been female comics throughout history who have beaten the odds in a variety of ways. And, as discussed, there are now far more women as well as people of color than ever before who are making inroads into the world of comedy entertainment. However, the newly developing visibility of women in comedy, including unapologetically feminist women, has brought the struggle over territory out into the open.

Institutional Changes

The comedy industry in the United States is one that has long been quite conservative and slow to change. Layered on top of all the existing cultural biases around gender roles has been a media and entertainment industry that was structurally rigid for a very long time. While many strains of comedic performance began (and continue) in live venues, including the vaudeville circuit and later comedy clubs (themselves rigidly controlled by each club's booker), by the 1950s, if one wanted to "make it" as a comedic performer, one had to break into television in some way. Television programming in the United States, particularly during the network era, was developed to appeal to as wide an audience as possible. The networks were ultimately beholden to advertisers, who were providing the money, and advertisers were jittery about associating their product with anything that might offend or otherwise challenge audience members. Consequently, there was very little appetite for overtly political or contentious material that would presumably alienate large swaths of the public. While there were flashes of satire within widely popular variety shows starting in the early 1960s, any harder-hitting satiric programs did not last long (Day 45–54). Relatedly, there was also little interest in defying audience expectations around gender roles or in deviating very far from proven formulas. This means, for instance, that Joan Rivers, who broke many barriers by simply being a female comedian (starting in the late 1950s) and who eventually became a popular guest host on *The Tonight Show* with Johnny Carson, was nevertheless not on the list of possible successors NBC drew up in preparation for Carson's retirement in 1991, a list that, according to Rivers, consisted of ten men (Kohen 147). Women simply were not late-night host material. Financial resources, network support, airtime, and performance venues were by and large controlled by powerful male industry players, limiting women's opportunities, while the institutional incentives led toward restricting the range of female bodies and viewpoints that did make it to air.

In recent years, many of these structures have undergone massive change. Beginning in the 1980s, the development of cable, satellite, and digital technologies, combined with changes in regulatory practices, irrevocably re-created the industry and fragmented audiences. Streaming platforms and the proliferation of screens further ushered in the era now referred to by television scholars as either "post network" or "post TV" (Lotz; Spigel). These changes fundamentally altered the economic structure of the television industry, incentivizing different programming strategies. Long gone are the days when a particular show could conceivably be watched by fully half of the country. Instead, the sheer number of programs created has exponentially increased, while each one can be aimed at much narrower taste cultures. Because platforms need not appeal to everyone, they can throw some money toward more specialized projects or take a chance on a more risky program than would have been conceivable just twenty years ago. Indeed, the streaming platform Netflix has built its reputation on being everything to everyone, not by creating blockbuster hits that the whole country is watching but by algorithmically recommending material to each consumer that is categorically similar to what they have already been watching. Those who like "edgy" comedy, or female stand-ups, or satire will see more of the same when they log into the platform; those who don't, almost certainly will not unless they expressly go digging. While audiences themselves have become far more self-selecting and insular, producers have much less worry about the potential divisiveness of a particular text, as it has become increasingly unlikely that viewers who would find a particular program upsetting would even be aware of its existence. Outside of the large platforms, increasing numbers of performers and writers are also building their own short-form material designed for video sharing sites like YouTube and TikTok. Some have found success without having to go through the usual industry gatekeepers. Individual performers in the comedy industry in particular are making use of social media (Slack feeds, Facebook pages, and Patreon meetups) to create ever more focused fan communities.

As part of the enormous expansion of content that has resulted, there has been a concurrent blurring of traditional genre boundaries. For instance, Geoffrey Baym describes the cross-pollination of the entertainment sphere with the political sphere as "discursive integration" (262), highlighting both the usage of entertainment techniques into the world of straight news and the incorporation of political discussion into comedy entertainment. As some of the old conceptions about which genres audiences will watch have faded away, there is now far more experimentation and play. The streaming platforms in particular can also produce much more politicized or otherwise divisive material. Thus, the amount of satire on television exploded in the aughts and 2010s, along with the development of more quirky comedies, raunchy material, and niche humor.

At the same time, some of the barriers to women's participation in the entertainment industry have come down. While the industry is still far from equitable, more women are gaining positions of influence both behind the scenes and as performers. Without all of the same restraints as in the past, many of these women are expressing feminist views or otherwise disobeying some of the old rules around how to be a woman in the public eye. As the old economic structures that propped up the discursive lines around gender roles in the industry have crumbled, one might assume that those discursive lines would likewise fade away. And while there certainly is some flux and change, as this book documents, people are also rushing to the ramparts to defend and strengthen those discursive lines or to define what will spring up in their place. The many battles over comedy routines documented in this volume are taking place in that vacated space. As Tomsett writes of the incursion of women into comedy, "the inclusion of women into this competitive and predominantly male industry has resulted in the crisis of male identity and a reassertion of traditional masculinity, now being played out through reactionary humour" ("Twenty-first Century Fumerist" 7). Ultimately, the backlash is not simply about the comedy industry but about what it means to be a woman in the public sphere.

Women and the Public Sphere

First developed by Jurgen Habermas, the "public sphere" is a theory about the circulation of public discourse and the competition of different worldviews within public culture. Habermas defines what he called "the bourgeois public sphere" as "the sphere of private people come together as a public" (27), pinpointing its development in the eighteenth-century coffeehouses of England and France, where individuals gathered for debate. In theory, all were to ignore the class and social backgrounds of the other speakers and to focus on whichever arguments were the strongest. Habermas argues that discussions of art and literature (newly accessible to the bourgeoisie) led to critiques of institutions such as the monarchy, eventually undercutting existing political systems and nurturing a critical press. In his telling, these public forums for political debate engendered the development of true public opinion. The concept of the public sphere has remained a popular ideal for theorists to return to, as it is held up as an essential condition if democracies are to function as democracies. However, most now take as a given that Habermas got a number of things wrong. First, while it would be nice to think that participants could simply ignore the social status and identities of other speakers, we know that has never actually been true, either then or now. Second, we now understand that there was never simply one unitary public sphere.

Theorists writing after Habermas have pointed out that women and poor people were not simply regrettably excluded from the coffee shops (as Habermas had argued); rather, the bourgeois men who saw themselves as creating a public sphere also deliberately developed elitist codes of conduct in order to distinguish their territory from other spheres, especially the feminine salon culture. In fact, the development of the public sphere was predicated on a newly structured division between the masculine public sphere and the feminine private sphere. Joan B. Landes explains "in their preferred version of the classical universe, bourgeois men discovered a flattering reflection of themselves—one that imagined men as properly political and women as naturally domestic" (4). That division set the stage for expectations around correct gendered behavior for centuries to come. As we explore in chapter 4, the domestic sphere was inextricably linked with the raising of children, including the moral instruction of the next generation. The purity and serenity of that home space was seen as miles removed from the roughness and crudeness of the public sphere. Women wanting to trespass too deeply into the public sphere were seen as enormously suspect, meaning that their femininity and virtue were themselves in question. The idealized wife and mother was someone who needed to be shielded from the vulgarity and meanness of public life (and, of course, to fail to become a wife and mother at all was to fail at bourgeois womanhood).

As a part of that division, there were concurrent behavioral norms and expectations. Landes quotes the editor of a popular news sheet in 1790s revolutionary France as observing that "it is no longer permitted to women to organize in clubs; they will be tolerated as spectators, silent and modest, in the patriotic societies" (145). This silence and modesty was crucial. When women did speak, they were to keep their voices soft and unobtrusive. As I explore in subsequent chapters, that expectation of women in public has been difficult to shake off. Despite it being more acceptable now for women to be active in public life and to seek public positions, they are still regularly pilloried for speaking too shrilly, aggressively, angrily, or crudely.

Of course, public life is now very different than it was in the eighteenth century. Of all the transformations, one of the most enormous has been the advent of the internet and digital social life more broadly. Some of the old methods of face-to-face deliberation still endure (think school board meetings and the like), but online communication has clearly become a hugely important part of public deliberation. As detailed by Sarah Sobieraj, "participatory online spaces such as comment sections, blogs, Facebook, Twitter, and YouTube now serve as digital public spheres in the sense that they provide a space for and include the practice of open discussion about matters of common concern" (7). These platforms potentially reach an almost unlimited number of interlocutors as well as silent observers/readers. As a consequence, there are now many more opportunities for individual people to become publicly visible than ever before. There are both advantages and liabilities to that increased visibility.

On the upside, it is now exponentially easier to communicate with others with whom one shares commonalities of interest, identity, or experience, no matter how narrow. In response to Habermas, Nancy Fraser articulated that because it is so difficult for individuals to put aside status differentials when debating with one another (meaning that the styles of communication favored by different groups become unequally valued) and because the dominant group inevitably sets the terms of what should be considered of interest to the public sphere, there have always been counterpublics "elaborating alternative styles of political behavior and alternative norms of public speech" (116). The difference between then and now, though, is that in the present day, members of even tiny counterpublics can be dispersed across the globe but still be engaged in ongoing conversation with one another. Thus, it is that much easier to create such discourse communities. Similarly, as we have touched on, a greater diversity of voices are receiving amplification through these platforms.

The corollary to this increased visibility, however, is the volatility and controversy that shadows the transgression of traditional boundaries. Visible, vocal women in public already challenge the norms of traditional femininity. And when they transgress further by seeking membership in smaller gate-kept subcultures that have traditionally been male-dominated—such as niche "nerd" cultures formed around video games or, more to our purpose, comedy—female participation is regularly met with open hostility. Indeed, "when a woman enters a space that is male-dominated and expects to be taken seriously, her mere presence is often interpreted as a challenge, regardless of intent" (Sobieraj 12). When women do intend to publicly shake things up, trespass across boundaries, or transgress against traditionally gendered norms, many view this as a declaration of war. In such cases, the women themselves then become sites of cultural contestation.

Cultural Contestation

Sarah Banet-Weiser has pointed out that while popular feminism has gained in visibility in contemporary culture, popular misogyny has gathered steam right alongside. As she explains, a broader cultural acceptance of feminism (even if it is a version of feminism that does not challenge deep structures of power), for some men "stimulates fear, trepidation, aggression, and violence" (2). This generalized backlash has coalesced into something of an organized movement or collection of movements with shared goals—namely, to challenge the public acceptance of feminist aims and to elevate traditional gender roles, including male dominance and female subservience. These movements are collectively now referred to as the "manosphere." While the varied communities that make up the manosphere might vary in their radicality (anywhere from simple misogyny to avowed aims of violence), the general collective focus is on countering feminist rhetoric and on hounding publicly vocal women online. As such, this movement inevitably plays a role in most of the case studies I examine in this book. In chapter 2 (focused on Leslie Jones and the *Ghostbusters* movie), we witness the rise of the manosphere as a powerful cultural force with the capability of setting the terms of the cultural conversation. In subsequent chapters, it is present but does not always manage to dominate the conversation in the same way.

Beyond the manosphere, however, all of the comedians in this book have attracted more generalized cultural attention, prompting journalists, politicians, celebrities, and citizens to weigh in on the various controversies (most of whom are unconnected to the manosphere). Here we have the volatility of female transgression meet the sudden centrality of the comedy industry as a cultural battleground. While, as discussed, there was some hand-wringing that attended the original popularity of satiric programs like *The Daily Show* and *The Colbert Report* related to worries that comedy programming was somehow cheapening political discourse, it has now become far more taken for granted that the comedy industry is political terrain, implicitly raising the stakes. Consequentially, comedy has come to be treated as a potentially important arena of influence.

Indeed, perhaps because professional and amateur comedy alike provide a space that allows for both irreverence and political speech, it has become a favored mode for political point scoring. As Maggie Hennefeld, Annie Berke, and Michael Rennett put it, "laughter is a tactic of rhetorical combat at the very front and center of the escalating culture wars in the United States (if not globally). Laughing at the Other—whether it is enabled by Rush Limbaugh or Sacha Baron Cohen, Milo Yiannopoulos, or Samantha Bee—has become a daily ritual that entrenches our tribalist political beliefs and ideological values" (141).

Perhaps no one has taken this reality to heart more than President Trump, who threw himself whole-heartedly into the midst of those culture wars from the very beginning of his first candidacy for president. In an insightful article in the *New York Times* following Trump's 2020 election loss, television critic James Poniewozik argues "with the election of President Trump, a pop-culture figure himself who intuited the connection between cultural fandom and political tribalism . . ., the political and culture-war wings of conservatism merged" (C4). As Poniewozik points out, the year he announced his candidacy, Trump also jumped into the pile on of people expressing outrage that the beloved comedic movie franchise *Ghostbusters* was being remade with all-female leads (a topic I explore in detail in chapter 2). In addition to taking umbrage over perceived slights to the conservative worldview within the entertainment world, as president, he was obsessed with what the professional comedians were saying about him, sometimes confusingly segueing from matters of state to complaints about the late-night comedy shows during a press conference.

Matt Meier reminds us that prior to running for president, Trump had plenty of experience in both reality television and the world of professional wrestling, making him quite at home in the realm of carnival (in reference to Bakhtin's concept). Meier argues that at least part of Trump's "rhetorical appeal is the construction of a carnival that positions him against the official power of the American media establishment" (9). While many outside of Trump's fan base initially regarded his penchant for affixing his adversaries with rude nicknames, for example, as simply vulgar and inappropriate, for his fans, it has often added to his appeal. As Meier puts it, "Whereas presidents tend to stay in the official realm of political seriousness and comedians keep to carnival, Trump's carnivalization of the office inverts the relationship as a means of containing the liberating force of carnival" (13). In other words, he is unwilling to cede the power of ridicule to the comedians. As Poniewozik explains of his first term, Trump did not, "like previous presidents attending the Kennedy Center honors or sharing a something-for-everyone Spotify playlist, see culture as a way to find common ground. He saw it as a battleground with winners and losers, and one full of opportunities to inflame divisions" (C4). While one could see Trump's thin skin for comedic slights and his own mean-spirited humor as somewhat pathetic, it does also reflect a canny understanding of comedy as a site of struggle; these are the types of battles that he has been arguably more focused on moment-to-moment than those being waged by the country's real-world troops.

And those battles (such as the *Ghostbusters* moment) are often undeniably gendered. Shortly after the dust had settled on the 2016 election between Trump and Hillary Clinton, Emily Nussbaum of the *New Yorker*, citing the warnings she thought that the television show *South Park* had given leading up to the election, argued that the fight between Trump and Clinton "could not be detached from the explosion of female comedy" ("How Do You Fight"). Trump, she explained, drew from the long history of male-dominated insult-comedy, while his "call to Make America Great Again was a plea to go back in time, to when people knew how to take a joke. It was an election about who owned the mike." Indeed, the gleefulness with which Trump rallygoers shouted slogans like "lock her up!" and "Trump that bitch" about Clinton demonstrates how many of Trump's fans relished the opportunity to vicariously tap into the thrillingly impolite territory of the male insult comic who just wants a chick to make him a sandwich.

Citing the smoldering fear and anger inflamed by the rise of popular feminism, Banet-Weiser argues that President Trump tapped right into that well of discontent, a task made particularly easy as he was pitted against the first viable female candidate for president. Indeed, "Trump presents himself (and his supporters see him) as being on a recuperative mission, a pursuit to restore patriarchy, to repair injuries caused by women, to return capacity to men" (177). Trump has a long track record of publicly attacking strong, outspoken women in very personal terms, particularly those whom he sees as threatening, often when they have confronted him with his own sexism or have otherwise dared to critique him (figures as disparate as Rosie O'Donnell, Megyn Kelly, and Hillary Clinton). Presumably, then, feminist comedy is something he would absolutely loathe. And, in fact, in chapter 4, we explore two controversies over routines by feminist comedians Michelle Wolf and Samantha Bee that revolved around members of the Trump administration. In both cases, the president and his spokespeople roundly condemned the comedy routines, labeling the comedians with words such as *filthy* and *disgusting*. This is not, however, a book about Trump. Rather, he happens to be symptomatic of larger cultural forces.

It is this book's contention that it is in the varied and conflicted reactions to the strong, outspoken, funny, sometimes vulgar comedians profiled here that we see society working out its divisions. While popular feminism has, as discussed, become highly visible of late and is certainly not exclusive to the realm of comedy, as Maggie Hennefeld argues, "the resurgence of feminism

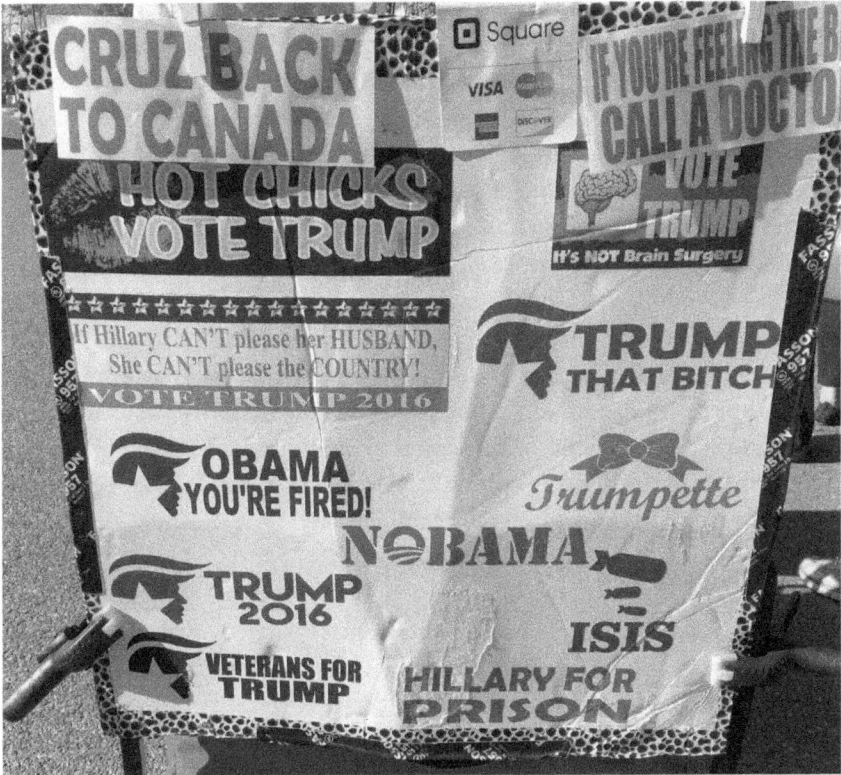

Figure 1.1. Many of Donald Trump's 2016 rallygoers seemed to relish Trump's flippant sexism and use of insult comedy.
Top: From James McNellis from Washington, DC, United States, CC BY 2.0 (https://creativecommons.org/licenses/by/2.0), via Wikimedia Commons.
Bottom: From Trump Rally #ShoreTrump [Photograph], by Forsaken Fotos, 2020, CC BY 2.0 (https://www.flickr.com/photos/55229469@N07/), via Flickr.

as a potent force in the battle to combat gender oppression and systemic discrimination is taking shape overwhelmingly (though not exclusively) through mainstream popular comedy" (87). Perhaps because comedy was an industry that was so hostile to female performers for so long, there is all the more urgency to articulate new comedic points of view now that the door is cracking open. And while there is clearly an eager audience for these new comedic performers, there are also many who are repulsed by some combination of the jokes and the individuals telling them. It is a clearly combustible mix: in feminist comedy, we have the contemporary awareness of comedy as political battleground meet the always visibleness of female cisgendered bodies and the contentiousness of women's voices. The result, as this book explores, is that feminist comedy becomes a site of near continual discursive struggle. Time and again, we find big and small cultural controversies and moments of societal introspection that have swirled, like the eye of a hurricane, over feminist comedians, making their bodies and voices the sites of public contestation. Sometimes these battles are over the nature of comedy itself, but as this book contends, if one digs below the surface, it becomes apparent that the disputes are at their core about much broader cultural issues, such as what is appropriate behavior for particular gendered and raced bodies, whose voices can be heard in what registers, and what topics may be discussed in the public sphere. Through the discourse around these newly visible comedians, we can often see the public working through ideals and boundaries in real time. We see both enlarged and expanded opportunities for cultural change as well as angry roadblocks around such changes. I have named each of the chapters that follow after particular affective states, because these feminist performers and their material seem to elicit strong emotional responses. These emotions rise to the surface of the ongoing cultural conversations, leaving tangible clues to the cultural shifts taking place below the surface.

Chapter Overviews

Chapter 2, "Ridicule," centers on one of the first instances of targeted trolling of women in the public eye that became widely visible to the general public. It details the deluge of slurs, insults, and threats directed at Leslie Jones following the release of the all-female reboot of the *Ghostbusters* franchise and the subsequent cultural conversation about what should be done in response to the harassment. Jones's treatment was rooted in misogynoir—the specific form of bias leveled at Black women in particular. This chapter fleshes out why the culture war battles that flare up around movies, video games, and other forms of popular culture should not be treated as petty squabbles but rather as struggles for power that have real and material effects. In this case, though there was some dismay about Jones's experience, the cultural conversation about why it was occurring and whether it was truly a problem was muddled and confused. Without widespread acknowledgment that the attacks stemmed from deep-rooted, systemic bias, society at large left open the door for that treatment to become a new norm rather than an aberration.

Chapter 3, "Loathing," focuses on comedian Amy Schumer and the loathing she has attracted from both the political Right and the Left. Schumer has produced a number of notable feminist sketches on her Comedy Central program *Inside Amy Schumer*. But as her notoriety has grown, so too has the hatred directed at her. Some of this has, as with Leslie Jones, been part of a coordinated attack by manosphere activists. But she is also intensely disliked by many Black feminists in particular who believe that her comedy is often racially insensitive. I argue that Schumer has in some sense become representative of white feminism itself—attacked by those who feel threatened by its visibility while also rightfully critiqued for its blind spots and often unacknowledged privilege. In the end, it is a position that will never be comfortable.

Chapter 4, "Revulsion," examines the two public controversies that occurred in quick succession in 2018 around the routines of two different comics: Michelle Wolf's monologue at the White House Correspondents' Association dinner and Samantha Bee's segment on the policy of separating children from their immigrant parents at the border, which contained a crude insult about Ivanka Trump. In the cultural conflagrations that resulted and the myriad voices that weighed in, there was a broad discursive struggle taking place over conceptions of femininity and motherhood and, ultimately, over how to be a woman in the public sphere. In both cases, defense of the jokes' victims revolved around their status as "wives and mothers," while disavowals of the joke tellers focused on the vulgarity of their use of profanity and sexual innuendo. It was also largely reduced to a "catfight" between the individual comedians and the female victims of their jokes, while the real issues and the substance of their critique dropped from view, particularly the injustices suffered by the immigrant families being forcibly separated at the border (the topic of Bee's segment) as well as the powerful men setting the policies in motion, demonstrating the ideological rerouting that occurs in public discussion when the focus remains on women's embodied behavior. Nevertheless, these twin controversies do provide examples of the way in which feminist comics are attempting to change these dynamics by pushing back against conceptions of what it means to be a woman in public.

Chapter 5, "Hope," is about Hannah Gadsby's comedy special *Nanette*. Prior to the release of *Nanette* on Netflix in 2018, Gadsby was relatively unknown outside of the Australian region. However, the special became enormously popular almost immediately, spread by both word of mouth and formal reviews. In *Nanette* Gadsby deconstructs their own set in order to reveal the trauma hidden behind their humorous stories. As it rose in cultural prominence, there was indeed some backlash, including complaints that the special was not actually comedy. However, the piece was also fiercely defended, not simply by a niche fan base, but by a wide swath of viewers, commentators, and reviewers. *Nanette* proved to be both cathartic and affecting for many. It spoke well to the moment as the world was coming to terms with the #MeToo movement, and it provided a new framework for processing trauma, hurt, and discrimination while calling into question business as usual within male-dominated industries like comedy and art. Though there are other niche performers and thinkers who have said similar things as Gadsby, Gadsby's special became an easily accessible node for identification as well as a conduit for a particular critique that many were clearly hungry to hear articulated. The enormous amount of attention and discussion generated by the piece reminds us that we need popular cultural touchstones through which to shift the conversation.

Finally, the conclusion pulls together all of the individual case studies, drawing links between the variety of public battles currently being waged by and around female performers and tracing what meaning is being made through them. In the conclusion, I follow up on the second or third acts of all of the featured performers and how the narratives around these figures continue to be shaped through a push and pull of public contention combined with the performers' own interventions.

The book takes a bird's-eye look at the larger culture wars, documenting where the fault lines lie and why conceptions about gender and race remain some of the most contentious and fraught. It concludes on why it is in and around feminist comedy that we see some of these battles at their most raw. These transgressive comedic voices are the book's focus, as these voices are themselves the sites of contestation. They provide powerful modes of broadening the public sphere while also engendering significant public discomfort and blowback.

2

Ridicule

Leslie Jones and the Growing Visibility of the Alt-Right

WHEN THE CAST of the *Ghostbusters* reboot was announced in early 2015, the complaints and preemptive condemnations began. While some commentators lamented that the original movies were so beloved that they should never be remade, the vast majority of the criticism focused on the fact that the main characters would all be women. The overwhelmingly male group of vocal superfans of the original franchise howled about the perceived desecration of their childhood memories. Most decided that the new film would be irretrievably awful while taking potshots at some of the better-known actresses in the cast. As Peter Cullen Bryan and Brittany R. Clark detail, in that early wave of complaints, "there is a clear animosity toward [Melissa] McCarthy in particular, with users attempting to fat-shame the actress, while also a retreading of the hoary 'women aren't funny' trope" (154). The anger continued to grow in the lead-up to the movie's release, becoming more intensely misogynist and, once the trailer was put out a year later, eventually including calls to action, as commenters encouraged others to actively try to tank the movie's ratings by giving it one-star reviews on IMDb and other user-generated review sites. This sentiment became far more targeted and decidedly nastier after the movie was finally released, in July 2016. That is when a scathing review written by Milo Yiannopoulos, then editor of the alt-right news site Breitbart, singled out cast member Leslie Jones as "the worst of the lot," leading to an instantaneous deluge of hate and harassment directed only at her. It was the first moment that this sort of targeted harassment really became visible to many in the culture (building on the #Gamergate controversy), sparking a great deal of cultural conversation about why it was happening, whether it was truly problematic, and what could possibly be done in response. This chapter aims to deconstruct both the harassment itself and the wider discussion that unfolded. That somewhat muddled conversation reveals a great deal about the cultural fissures around both race and sex.

Leslie Jones began her performing career in stand-up comedy before joining *Saturday Night Live* in 2014, first as a writer and then as a cast member. The casting call for a Black female comedian that resulted in her hiring at *SNL* was the result of heated public criticism the year before about the overwhelming whiteness of the program's cast and the complete dearth of Black women on the show. Jones became the oldest person ever to join the cast when she made her debut at forty-seven. Jones also appeared in a film directed by Chris Rock that same year and then played a cameo role in Amy Schumer's 2015 film *Trainwreck*. By the time *Ghostbusters* was released in 2016, Jones's star was rising, though she was perhaps not yet as widely recognizable as the movie's other three stars. Indeed, it is likely that many of her tormentors were unfamiliar with her as a performer before being alerted to the campaign to trash the *Ghostbusters* movie. Nevertheless, as we will see, members of the manosphere gleefully piled on once the call went out.

While her harassment on Twitter attracted a great deal of attention, there was plenty of disagreement about whether it was ultimately significant and if celebrities should simply be prepared for such treatment if they are to be in the public eye. For some, while the attacks may have been distasteful, they were a distraction from more consequential matters. Indeed, when then-candidate Trump felt the need to express his distaste for the idea of a female *Ghostbusters* reboot, commentators on the left scoffed at him for making pronouncements about trivial popular cultural disputes. However, making such announcements was entirely strategic, a way to anoint himself as the lead knight in the culture wars. As James Poniewozik says of Trump's statement, "'Now they're making "Ghostbusters" with only women. What's going on!' was a way of telling men that he would protect them from becoming superfluous" (C4). Similarly, the harassment subsequently meted out to Jones was not simply an unfortunate instance of overzealous fandom. Rather, it was a coordinated effort to squash Black women's influence. I argue that it would be folly to minimize these clashes or to treat culture war skirmishes around entertainers and popular culture as somehow peripheral from real political debates and struggles. It is important that we recognize that these are absolutely battles over real material resources and social and political power. Further, the lack of meaningful action around cases such as Jones's leads to such harassment becoming a cultural norm, one more barrier to success for women and people of color.

I begin the book with this particular case study for several reasons. Jones's treatment was one of the first instances of targeted gendered harassment that registered at the level of popular culture, becoming part of the cultural consciousness and thus the wider conversation. As such, we can see people truly working out their feelings about this treatment in dialogue with one another. And, sadly, we can also see how the public's failure to mount any concentrated effort to address the phenomenon set the stage for continued apathy and inaction.

Female-Centered Entertainment and Online Harassment

One of the enduring staple film genres in the Hollywood tradition is the buddy comedy. Two or more friends (or seeming enemies) are on some sort of adventure together. They are typically a mismatched team who must learn to cooperate or appreciate one another while getting into all sorts of hijinks along the way. Historically, buddy films have been almost exclusively about men, with women pushed to the margins of the narrative as we focus on the male friendship. There have been some notable female-driven exceptions, including films like *Thelma and Louise* (1991) and *Outrageous Fortune* (1987), but female buddy movies have clearly been a harder sell for studio executives. Romantic comedies could already reliably capture the female and date-night market, but female buddy comedies were a swing into more uncharted territory. Thus, when the film *Bridesmaids* came out in 2011, it was hailed by many (perhaps hyperbolically) as a feminist milestone. While it did center on a wedding (more typical for a rom-com), it was primarily about female friendship; it featured a cast of quirky female characters, and it used the comedic talents of its cast to very funny, raunchy effect. The director, Paul Feig, went on to direct another successful female buddy comedy, *The Heat*, a couple years later and then took on *Ghostbusters*.

Given those previous successes, the *Ghostbusters* project likely did not seem like a particularly edgy choice. However, the fact that it was a reboot of a very popular franchise upped the stakes for many. Additionally, as we will explore further, at that point, "men's rights" groups, antifeminist groups, and others were becoming increasingly networked online, creating community with one another by picking enemies to destroy together. The fact that *Brides-maids* had received so much praise, while its stars (including two who would also star in *Ghostbusters*, Kristin Wiig and Melissa McCarthy) were praised for beating the raunchy male comedians at their own game, had also likely raised hackles. Finally, aggrieved male fans had recently very publicly flexed their muscles in attacks on high-profile women in the video game industry, demonstrating their power as a group.

Approximately a year before the *Ghostbusters* cast was publicly announced, the type of targeted harassment, threats, and bullying that Jones ended up receiving began being directed at several female video game developers and video game journalists. Mostly male video game enthusiasts were upset about the creation of nontraditional video games—for instance, one called *Depression Quest*, created by Zoe Quinn, that takes players into the experience of someone who is battling depression. After her game received positive reviews, Quinn was deluged with rape and death threats. These later escalated to an astonishing level when her ex-boyfriend published a blog piece in which he made unsubstantiated accusations that she had gotten the good reviews because of a sexual relationship with a journalist. After her digital accounts were hacked and her address published online, she felt that she had to leave her home. Quinn's harassers dubbed the supposed scandal around her positive publicity "#Gamergate." The campaign soon grew to also target a feminist media critic who wrote about video games (Anita Sarkeesian) and another female game developer (Brianna Wu). All three figures had to cancel public events and to temporarily leave their homes out of fear for their safety. As Emma Jane explains, the campaign "perfectly demonstrates the slippage between contemporary anti-fandom and outright misogyny, harassment, and violence" (56). The Gamergate movement did not have any official leaders or manifestos, but it was able to focus and weaponize an enormous degree of gendered anger and resentment. Those participating in the harassment often spoke vaguely about defending journalism ethics or about opposing political correctness in gaming culture. As Amanda Philips explains, these sorts of attacks are a direct reaction to the growing visibility of "women, queer folks, and people of color in the gaming community." The battle is "between gamers who attempt to expand the industry's representational and cultural practices and those who try to silence them with hate speech, death and rape threats, and other forms of harassment" (27–28). Those doing the harassing see themselves as defending sacred territory from desecration by invaders. We should be clear that what they object to is women and people of color transgressing into traditionally white, male space.

There was a fair amount of (often bemused) news coverage of Gamergate; although some raised alarm bells that this didn't bode well, many of the articles treated it as a nastily aberrant phenomenon that would not repeat itself (Thier) or as a story about the internal dynamics within that strange niche subculture of gaming (what are those crazy geeks up to now?) rather than as a disturbing new normal. However, when the fire hose of harassment was turned on Leslie Jones and the *Ghostbusters* movie, it more noticeably entered the world of mainstream popular culture. Many who might never follow what was happening in the gamer world were at least dimly aware of what was happening with the big movie releases and knew that there was a brewing movement against the new *Ghostbusters*. By the time that the harassment was turned on Jones, the phenomenon had reached the level of popular cultural controversy.

As Bryan and Clark detail, the outrage over a female-centered reboot grew from the presumption of a larger agenda lurking behind our entertainment and of the "idea that a film starring women must be made only for women, and that the previous audience could no longer see themselves in the characters, and as such were no longer the target audience of a previously beloved property" (154). Taking place as #Gamergate was continuing to unfold, participants rallied each other toward turning their sense of collective grievance into a coordinated movement, casting it in terms of cultural erasure, a zero-sum game in which greater visibility of women and minorities equated to an attack on white men, on geek culture, and on tradition, an attack that needed to be countered at all costs. Thus, "the narrative that emerges is one of a culture war between the genders, with *Ghostbusters* a valiant last stand, at least until the next last stand occurs" (156). Indeed, by opening day, the film's trailer had "earned the moniker of being the most disliked movie trailer on YouTube, and the trailer's comment section exploded to include nearly 240,000 comments" (Showalter et al. 83). Those numbers were, of course, not accidental but the result of a concerted effort by disgruntled antifans intent on sabotaging the movie while connecting with other like-minded men. Even before the campaign focused on Leslie Jones, many of the online comments were both graphic and violent. Dana Showalter, Shannon Stevens, and Daniel L. Horvath describe the snowballing commentary as a form of "homosocial bonding" (15), as the (mostly) male commentators egged each other on with increasingly offensive posts. They explain that "this form of bonding, not uncommon in the comment section, includes both a consistent escalation of violent misogynist rhetoric and the use of toxic masculinity to uphold patriarchal communicative power" (96). The bonding occurs over the ever-more outrageous insults and threats, each new commenter gleefully one-upping the last as part of a collectively played game.

That bubbling stew of resentment and self-righteousness had reached a fever pitch before the movie's opening day, when provocateur Milo Yiannopoulos helped focus the crowd's ire by writing a scathing review of the film for Brietbart. Though he (unsurprisingly) disparages the movie as a whole, his most disdainful critique is aimed at Leslie Jones in particular. Jones was arguably the least well known of the primary cast members at the time and was, notably, the only actress of color of the four protagonists. Yiannopoulos asserts that in this film, "the enemy is all men, while the government ends up playing dad. Every man in the movie is a combination of malevolent and moronic." He goes on to say that the movie "seems to have been conceived entirely out of spite" (presumably against men) but that it is also "remarkably unkind to its female leads." Referring to the other leads as "fat," "clownish," and "repellant," he singles out Jones's character, Patty, as the worst, describing her as "worthy of a minstrel show" and stating, "The actress is spectacularly unappealing, even relative to the rest of the odious cast. But it's her flat-as-a-pancake black stylings that ought to have irritated the SJWs. I don't get offended by such things, but they should" (SJW stands for "social justice warrior," a term used disparagingly by the alt-right to describe political progressives). He then released a series of tweets that were made to appear as if they were from Jones herself, many of which contained racist language. Yiannopoulos had, by this point, developed a sizable fan base, largely by stoking the fires of #Gamergate. The reaction to his review was almost instantaneous.

Legions of Yiannopoulos's followers took to Twitter to assail Jones with racist and sexist insults, pornography, and racist memes. Overwhelmed by the deluge of hate, Jones screenshotted some of the worst examples and made them visible to her followers in order to draw attention to what was happening. Yiannopoulos also kept posting from the fake account that purported to be Jones's own. A day later, when the vitriol had only increased, Jones temporarily left Twitter. In response to Jones's public calls for Twitter to do something about the situation, the company announced that it was permanently banning Yiannopoulos and, shortly thereafter, creating a "quality filter" to help prevent harassment. Though Jones returned to Twitter, about a month later, her personal website was hacked and used to display photos of her driver's license and passport as well as stolen nude photos of her. The hack was widely seen as retaliation for Yiannopoulos's Twitter suspension.

Both #Gamergate and the anti-*Ghostbusters* campaign harnessed the masses of men involved with what is now referred to as the "manosphere," the growing array of groups online promoting some combination of men's rights activism, antifeminism, and misogyny. While these incidents made the existence of the manosphere more visible, it had been steadily developing as internet connectivity grew. As Sarah Banet-Weiser describes, "hundreds of websites and social media platforms are dedicated to opining, training, and expressing the urgency of the 'alpha male' in a landscape apparently emasculated by feminism in particular and by women in general" (116). She explains that the issues of the manosphere cover a range of topics: "from the more moderate, such as support for father's rights and custody rights, doubts over the prevalence of domestic violence, and reflexive support of the military, to the more extreme, such as normalizing rape and sexual violence, manipulating and controlling women into sex, and making death threats against a vast number of people (mostly women) who disagree with these views" (117). There is also plenty of overlap between the manosphere and the alt-right as well as other extreme right-wing adherents, most of whom espouse some anxiety about the dissolution of traditional gender roles. Milo Yiannopoulos, for instance, would certainly be described as a spokesperson for both the manosphere and the alt-right.

The wide array of formal groups and niche online communities that we could point to as part of the manosphere are not formally connected to one another; rather, as Showalter, Stevens, and Horvath put it, it is "a social space created by the reflexive circulation of discourse" (180). Building on Michael Warner's description of publics as entities created only through the repeated circulation of texts, they explain that the manosphere is continuously "created and re-created through the circulation of discourses about neomasculinity and anti-feminism, about movies that ruin men's childhood and present-day lives, the polite online conversations and vile anonymous comments, the professional reviews and the vernacular film criticism entries, the YouTube comments and the down votes, the Twitter wars and the terrorizing campaigns" (181). In other words, the gleefully offensive pictures and slurs sent to Leslie Jones do not exist in a vacuum; rather, they are continuous with more polite forms of discourse that circulate in society. It should also be noted that Jones's harassment "mirrors a world that is especially hostile to women of color. White men have historically weaponized rape and threats of rape to colonize and demoralize people of color" (99). While the more flamboyant reaches of the manosphere produce the most concentrated, toxic manifestations of cultural misogyny and racism, they simply offer up the most unabashed and well-organized threads of discourses that have long circulated throughout culture.

Misogynoir and the Culture Wars

In the public discussion of Jones's harassment, most acknowledged the racism behind the attacks. Indeed, the repeated motif of comparing Jones to the gorilla Harambe (who had recently been in the news after a child fell into his enclosure at a Cincinnati zoo) made the racism difficult to explain away. But there was far less discussion about the specificity of the harassment centered more precisely on her identity as a Black woman. The combination of sexism and racism experienced by Black women is a phenomenon referred to by Moya Bailey as "misogynoir." Bailey explains that the term "describes the uniquely co-constitutive racialized and sexist violence that befalls Black women as a result of their simultaneous and interlocking oppression at the intersection of racial and gender marginalization" (1). The specificity of that experience is neither analogous to the racism experienced by Black men nor the sexism experienced by white women. Bailey describes a number of harmful caricatures of Black women that have historically and contemporarily circulated in the media (figures like the Jezebel, mammy, Sapphire, and welfare queen), arguing that these caricatures "materially impact the lives of Black women by justifying poor treatment throughout all areas of society and throughout US history" (2). Jones's treatment in 2016 seems to fit squarely into this paradigm.

Of all the comedians profiled in this book, Jones is arguably the least explicitly political in her comedy. She had one sketch (her first on *Saturday Night Live*) that attracted criticism from some within the Black community, but otherwise she does not normally produce purposefully edgy or controversial content. In fact, in an interview with Van Jones, she explained that there was perhaps too much pressure for comedians to do topical or satirical material and that she prefers to just focus on making people laugh. After leaving *Saturday Night Live*, her gigs have included television commentary for several rounds of Olympic Games and the hosting job for the rebooted game show *Supermarket Sweep*, both aimed at a very broad audience. It is clear that it is not the content of Jones's material that has attracted the ire of antifans; rather, it is Jones herself. Not only is she a Black female comedian achieving some public success, but she is loud and outspoken. She is also six feet tall and broad-shouldered and has a short, often spiky haircut. As Katja Antoine explains, "Jones is not feminine by a white Western aesthetic, nor is she feminine by an aesthetic that exotifies dark-skinned women. Her appearance challenges such hegemonic images of womanhood. Her behavior also 'fails' to reproduce any acceptable versions of 'authentic' femininity. What's more, she's not trying to" (43). Instead, she deliberately takes up space, goggles her eyes, or throws back her head with raucous laughter. Speaking specifically about Jones's stand-up and sketch comedy, Antoine argues that her "unapologetic in-your-face attitude and physicality on stage are provocative before she even opens her mouth. She does not present herself as racially palatable and does not seek to placate any audience discomfort that may result; rather, she seems to revel in it" (42).

This idea of racial palatability seems key. Jones does not try to modulate her stage persona for white audiences. Indeed, the salience of race to Jones's performance in the *Ghostbusters* movie was the element that Yiannopoulos zeroed in on in his original review, as he referred to her "flat-as-a-pancake black stylings" and quipped that the Left should be offended. In other words, he sees Jones through the prism of existing stereotypes of Black women—perhaps the loud and angry Sapphire character. Yiannopoulos essentially projected his own bigoted distaste for attention-grabbing Black women back onto Jones as a performer to allege that she herself was somehow inviting his racism. This logic of blaming Jones for her own abuse was then echoed one-thousand-fold in the crowd-sourced cruelty that Yiannopoulos's review engendered. Much of the invective was focused on her appearance, as posters implied that she was some combination of unattractive, masculine, or animalistic. The insults were consistently aimed at her embodiment as both Black and female, and the trolls seemed incensed that she was somehow flaunting her deviance from their personal ideals of womanhood. The fact that she had also been given a lead comic role in a high-profile movie further enflamed the resentment. Here misogynoir combined with the long-standing antipathy toward female comedians, already aroused by the presumption that the female ghostbusters were somehow desecrating the original movie. While the prerelease ire at the movie had been spread diffusely at everyone involved with the project, once Yiannopoulos aimed attention at Jones, she became the only target that mattered. As Danielle Fuentes Morgan points out, "women of color in particular are at a larger risk of having their texts and performances to be assumed too niche to succeed, or having their performances assumed to be inherently unrelatable for large swaths of the population" (140). Perhaps unsurprisingly, then, Jones came to personify the idea that the new *Ghostbusters* movie was not addressed to white men.

The type of vitriol directed at Jones, similar to that directed at the women of #Gamergate, is sometimes excused as antifandom criticism that is maybe overzealous. In fact, the power of such hate speech "lies in its insidious insistence that it is one thing (e.g., harmless commentary on a film) when it is actually something else (e.g., violent misogyny and racial vilification)" (Jane 56). Naked hate speech is frowned on; however, cultural commentary is something we wish to protect, and as we will see, framing such harassment as an issue of free speech has repeatedly succeeded in muddying the public discussion. But such hate speech has material effects.

As Eugenia Siapera argues, online misogyny that targets "prominent women associated with technology, feminism and the political sphere is important because it functions as paradigmatic misogyny: its outcome is not only to symbolically punish and silence these prominent women but also to discipline and deter all other women witnessing these attacks" (26). Siapera takes issue with the framing of this sort of harassment as part of the online culture wars, as she thinks it elides the stakes of what is happening, which is "the continued exclusion of women from accessing and controlling the means of production and from full socio-economic participation in the emerging new formation," which she refers to as "techno-capitalism" (21). I think she is entirely right that these attacks are about control of material resources and power and, indeed, that that is the intent behind them. However, I don't think that means we should cease speaking about them in terms of the "culture wars." Rather, I think it is all the more important that we do use that term while being clear about what it means.

Fighting the culture wars should not imply that because they are fought in and through forms of entertainment or popular culture, the stakes are trivial. On the contrary, that simply makes the battlefield more accessible for the average warrior. While the ordinary individual might not necessarily have much traditional political or economic power, most do have access to social media accounts and have the cultural capital to speak at length about Hollywood movies, comedy routines, or video games. By channeling collective energy into trying to intimidate and chase away female performers, they can attempt to ensure that "women's labour is stolen or denied, their knowledge and contributions ridiculed and denigrated, and . . . women's virtual bodies are banned from certain online spaces, just as women were once banned from the public sphere" (39). While the existing cultural bias that leads us to assume that popular culture is somehow insignificant allows for such struggles to be dismissed as petty squabbling over minutia, they are indeed about the allocation of resources and the replication of power structures. And the fact that they are attached to texts and issues that many find accessible makes them more easily used as a recruitment tool.

To those who piled on to Jones on Twitter, she was seen as fair game for a number of infractions (whether these were explicitly articulated or not): for trespassing into male territory, for trespassing into white territory, and for not conforming to white beauty ideals. As Angela Onwuachi-Willig puts it, "the harassment Jones faced was designed to signal to her that she was unequal to the men her harassers believed should have been in her movie role, and to undermine her actual performance of her job—here, the promotion of her movie" (114). While the makers of the *Ghostbusters* film were to get the message that an all-female cast was *not* what fans of the franchise wanted, Jones more specifically was to get the message that she herself did not deserve to be in the public eye.

The Film

In every other case study profiled in this book, the details of a comic's performance are what are under the microscope in the varied controversies and debates. When it comes to *Ghostbusters* and Jones's harassment, however, the nuances of the script and the specifics of Jones's acting are strangely almost beside the point. Yiannopoulos's review and the Twitter pile-on that ensued happened before the vast majority of participants could possibly have seen the movie itself (while many of those harassing Jones had pledged to never see it). Nevertheless, I think it is important to consider the particulars of the movie in question.

To be clear, the film was relatively typical of a high-profile reboot. The plot was updated and refocused but hit many of the same beats as the original. Like the original, it began just before the group of ghostbusters comes together as such, precipitated by one of them being fired from a professorship at Columbia University. After some smaller-scale ghost encounters, the team uncovers a plot to open a spirit portal that unleashes an apocalyptic attack on the city of New York, culminating in a giant sky scraper–sized ghost and its many minions wreaking temporary havoc on the city as the ghostbusters go to battle to take them down and set things right. There are also some fun cameos by cast members from the first movie as well as some other winking allusions to please the nostalgic fans. Like the original, the film is built around a stable of A-list comedic actors who are given the space to develop character-based comedy together, interspersed with a few spookier bits and some action sequences. While this is certainly a subjective judgment, I found the movie enjoyable and the comedy amusing. There is nothing groundbreaking about the movie, but it is an entertaining buddy film with a strong cast. Of course, if one does not like the performers (perhaps if one does not think women can or should be funny), one would get less enjoyment from this film. For their part, the professional reviews almost always opened with some bemused or critical reference to the sexist blowback the film had received, followed by the summation that the movie was just fine—not outstanding, but perfectly diverting or, in the words of Mahnola Dargis of the *New York Times*, "a movie that is a lot of enjoyable, disposable fun."

Yiannopoulos's assertion that the movie is antimen certainly does not hold up. Like in a male buddy comedy that focuses on the central players with women relegated to the sidelines, the men are secondary characters. As in most comedies, the characters are all quirky, though none of the men, with the clear exception of the central villain, are painted as malevolent. However, the *Ghostbusters* script does slyly nod to the controversy that had been brewing around the movie from the time of its casting. When Kristen Wiig's character, Erin, is directed to look at some of the reports of ghost sightings that have been sent to them, she inadvertently scrolls to the wrong online comment, which reads "ain't no bitches going to hunt no ghosts." A little later, she is reminded by Melissa McCarthy's character, Abby, that "you are not supposed to listen to what crazy people write in the middle of the night online." This is the closest that the film gets to calling men out for their treatment of women.

As for Jones herself, she plays the role of Patty Tolan, an MTA worker who is chased by a ghost in the subway tunnel and who visits the first three ghostbusters to help make sense of it. After the three spend the day with her and are themselves attacked by the same ghost, they agree to let her join the group due to her extensive knowledge of the history of the city and her interest in the project. Jones's performance in the film is strong. She does not grandstand as some comics do when transitioning to acting work; rather, she creates a believable character who helps further the storyline. Notably, while I've described Jones's style of comedy on *Saturday Night Live* and in her stand-up

Figure 2.1. Leslie Jones plays Patty Tolan in the 2016 film *Ghostbusters*. Here she is attempting to ignore the demon perched on her shoulders.

as often deliberately loud and exuberant, her portrayal of Patty is quite subdued in comparison. And while hers is the only primary character without an advanced degree, the script respects her intelligence, even having Abby yell out "Patty, you are a genius" when she figures out how to finally close the portal to the underworld in the film's climactic moments. She is in no way set up as a racial stereotype, as Yiannopoulos implies, nor is her performance somehow demeaning, as he hints when he describes it as "worthy of a minstrel show."

Interestingly, the film has one moment when it does point to Jones's difference. The ghostbusters have chased a number of demons out of the basement of a concert hall and onto the stage during a heavy metal show. To get from the stage to the back of the auditorium, Abby (McCarthy) flings herself into the arms of the audience, as she crowd-surfs to where she wants to go. Patty tries to do the same, but when she jumps off the stage, the audience does not reach out to catch her, meaning that she falls flat on her back onto the ground. As the room grows silent, she yells, "OK, I don't know if it was a race thing or a lady thing, but I'm mad as hell." Here the film tries to playfully (and perhaps inadequately) gesture to her differential treatment. Looking back, it now seems oddly prophetic, though the film of course could not anticipate the depths of the animosity to be leveled at Jones herself.

The Conversation

The harassment Jones received was so intense that it did become an object of wider cultural conversation, attracting the attention of many who were otherwise not all that interested in the *Ghostbusters* movie. Many watching from the sidelines were uncomfortable with the excesses of the harassment. However, the public generally struggled to define what the issues were and why or if they mattered.

The fact that there was bias of some sort directed at Jones was fairly legible to onlookers, but of precisely what kind was squishier for many. In the discussion that unfolded, the racism of the attacks was frequently acknowledged but not the sexism or, hence, the specificity of misogynoir. As Onwuachi-Willig explains, the fact that Jones's harassment did not involve sexual advances led to a "narrow understanding of her experiences as solely racial harassment by some writers and pundits" (114). This was despite the fact that the content of the messages she received contained clear references to both gender and race and that they included material such as photoshopped pictures of the performer with semen on her face. However, Onwuachi-Willig postulates that "the racialized nature of the harassment seemingly made it difficult for white women to see themselves in Jones, and accordingly, to see her experiences as related to sex" (113). Likely for that reason, there was not a noticeable outcry on Jones's behalf from white feminists.

In a discourse analysis study of the online reactions to the Leslie Jones attacks, Caitlin E. Lawson found that the most dominant theme of responses on Twitter consisted of messages of support, but "within this deluge of support, several women of color pointed out that key voices were missing or muted: white women" (823). Further, "when white women and men did show support, they were disproportionately praised across media platforms. The stars who got the most headlines for speaking out against Jones's harassers were Katy Perry, Dan Aykroyd, and Hillary Clinton" (823), despite the fact that far more Black stars overall had spoken up.

In an attempt to study how online harassment directed at Black women is processed by online communities, Stephanie Madden and colleagues found that it was when discussions turned to beauty standards that online discussants demonstrated an understanding of the intersectional forms of oppression that were at play. Some commenters pointed out that Jones's appearance made her more vulnerable to online attack, as her Afrocentric features marginalize her in an industry that privileges Eurocentric beauty ideals. However, the study also found that "commenters repeatedly referenced other Black celebrities as counterpoints to the argument, comparing Jones to well-known Black women like Kerry Washington, Oprah Winfrey, and Michelle Obama, and their treatment in public forums" (84). The authors note that "though their point was likely to highlight inequality in the public eye, the reassertion of figures who uphold traditional beauty standards (and the comparison to those who do not) also functions to reiterate and cement those standards" (84). In other words, though some of the basic critique behind the concepts of intersectionality and misogynoir are trickling into public discourse, the discussion itself often still inadvertently reinforces misogynoir.

Within the larger discussion, there was another prominent thread that served to minimize or excuse some of the abuse. This thread focused on Jones's status as a celebrity. As Madden and colleauges found, "many online commenters were unsympathetic to Jones' online abuse because, as one commenter posted, 'any celebrity on Twitter is literally asking for it'" (75). The logic here seems to be that attention and animus is the price one must be prepared to pay for fame and fortune. Jones's social class (as celebrity) is made to trump all other aspects of her identity, implicitly minimizing the specificity of the abuse linked to both race and sex. One of the effects of such discussion is a papering over of the wildly different forms of treatment meted out to different celebrities. What becomes easily elided is the fact that though someone like Tom Hanks receives plenty of attention (some negative), he presumably does not regularly receive pictures of himself with semen on his face.

In the aforementioned comment, sympathy is withheld from Jones both because of her status as a celebrity and her usage of the platform of Twitter. Here the argument is that since we know that there is a lot of ugly stuff on Twitter, it shouldn't come as a surprise to anyone who puts themselves out there. That sort of argument is one that shades easily into the position taken by those on the alt-right and in the manosphere—the communities responsible for the abuse.

Once Twitter began to respond to Jones's plea that the company do something about what was happening to her, the alt-right largely successfully painted the dispute as one over the freedom of speech and letting the market decide. As Viveca Greene puts it, platforms like Twitter create "the fiction of equality: one person one account. Donald Trump and a young Black feminist have the same accounts, and the only difference is the number of followers. Success or failure is measured in quantified market terms, and the neoliberal logic of 'let the market decide'" ("All They Need Is Lulz" 58). If Jones was complaining, the thinking goes, it is because she is a sore loser. When public sympathy swung in Jones's direction and when Yiannopoulos was suspended from Twitter, the alt-right howled that his speech had been unfairly censored and that the entire group was being victimized. As Lawson explains, this allowed them to "flip the discourse and frame themselves as oppressed and disadvantaged" (819). Indeed, the more that people online defended Jones or expressed upset over her treatment, the more the alt-right and members of the manosphere could paint themselves as under attack. Yiannopoulos pointed to the widespread circulation of feminist-inflected discourses (such as body positivity) as evidence that conservative thought was being bullied out of the public sphere. Once Twitter announced that it was suspending him, he proclaimed that they were targeting him for his conservative beliefs. As Lawson argues, he deliberately "mistakes discursive power for structural change" (828), asserting the dominance of feminism (as evidenced by public sentiment) despite the continued material advantages still held by white men in particular. Thus, for many, the conversation shifted away from one focused simply on online abuse and hate speech toward one about the perils of online censorship and about media moguls distorting the marketplace of ideas. This effectively muddied the conversational waters, making it appear that the issues were perhaps irredeemably complex. To be clear, however, when the alt-right argues for letting only the market decide whose speech to support, that is another way of arguing for majority rule and against the protection of minority voices. In this case, it also means providing individuals no protections from harassment and abuse.

While there was plenty of discussion of what had happened to Jones, the conversation did not evidence any cultural ability or willingness to do anything about it beyond some asking Twitter to step in, though Twitter's subsequent attempt to censure Yiannopoulos was itself not universally popular. Even if it had been, however, keeping the focus on what Twitter is or is not doing is its own form of deflection. It implies that the problem is a narrow one, perhaps a wonky issue with the algorithm, rather than an endemic cultural problem of rampant bias and discrimination. Instead, the public debated if the treatment was truly problematic or could be explained away for any number of good reasons or if it was a regrettable outcome of the marketplace of ideas. There was certainly no widespread acknowledgment of misogynoir or its effects. That lack of cultural introspection of course allows such mistreatment to continue not as an aberration but as its own sort of norm. And when it is framed as antifandom or cultural critique, it permits individuals to see themselves as righteous in defending their positions and piling on to their targets. As Jonathan Gray explains, "in a 'postracial,' 'postfeminist' world in which racism and sexism have supposedly disappeared, we should expect to find all sorts of racism and sexism taking the more publicly acceptable form of denigrating texts associated with people of color and women. We should also expect more complex (and some more progressive) dislikes of people to be expressed as dislikes of 'their' texts" (33). This again demonstrates the stakes of the culture wars, disputes that are routinely dismissed as petty bickering over popular culture. Those disputes are at the dead center of our ongoing power struggles around race and gender, and they have very real material effects on the lives of individuals, particularly the lives of women of color whose visibility in the public sphere is routinely seen as its own form of provocative transgression.

3

Loathing

Amy Schumer and White Feminism

COMEDIAN AMY SCHUMER is an interesting figure because she is hated by such a wide range of people. Though she is still undeniably a successful comedian, the insults about her online (emanating from a wide variety of sources) are so prolific and pervasive they are quite impossible to avoid. In one famous sketch on her program *Inside Amy Schumer*, she enlists a slew of famous actors to repeat ad nauseum some of the tamer (television-friendly) insults about her appearance, like "muppet tits" or "potato face," comically highlighting the hostility she elicits. Schumer began her career to plaudits for her ability to appeal to a variety of audience members and did indeed ride a wave of commercial and critical success that lifted her to celebrity status quite quickly. However, as her fame increased, she also generated a reaction from a sizable number of onlookers that can only be described as loathing. Strikingly, this loathing is emanating from several very different corners. On the one hand, she has become a favored target of the manosphere and the alt-right, which has trickled out into the more mainstream audience, partially because of the material she has produced from an unabashed feminist perspective and partially because she is seen as not quite skinny or flawless enough for the confidence she exudes. On the other hand, she has also received a great deal of criticism from women of color in particular for racial insensitivity in her comedy. As Jason Zinoman puts it in the *New York Times*, "She has become a lightning rod, taking criticism from all corners of the internet, periodically finding herself at the bottom of a pile-on." Ultimately, as I argue, Schumer has become representative of white feminism[1] and its attempts to infiltrate the male-dominated comedy industry. As such, she is despised by those threatened by feminism's visibility while being critiqued for mainstream feminism's blind spots and often unacknowledged privilege. For these reasons, the discussion about Schumer reveals all the cultural and political fissures surrounding feminism in the current moment.

Schumer began her career as a stand-up comedian and actor, first attracting industry attention during a run on the program *Last Comic Standing* in 2007. She further turned heads during the 2011 Comedy Central roast of Charlie Sheen, in which she came out swinging, clearly surprising the other performers, who were all relatively unfamiliar with her. In 2013, her sketch comedy program *Inside Amy Schumer* (*IAS*) debuted on Comedy Central, giving her significant name recognition. Her notoriety then exploded in 2015 due to the simultaneous release of the film *Trainwreck*, which she wrote and starred in, as well as the more unabashedly feminist third season of *IAS*, which garnered a great deal of praise from critics.

Schumer's comedy and persona has become a site of battle in the culture wars in a somewhat different manner than the turf guarding and misogynoir that greeted Leslie Jones with *Ghostbusters*. Schumer's case reveals the ways in which white feminism, in particular, signifies across diverse social groups. As discussed in the introduction, *feminism* is itself a contested term, one that is filled in radically differently by different constituencies. For members of the manosphere, Schumer began her career as an appealing sex object, a young, blonde, white woman who seemed to unproblematically fit the entertainment-world ideal but who soon revealed her feminist allegiances as well as her unwillingness to consistently comply with the beauty norms for female celebrities and, worse, her delight in telling jokes about her body's debasement. As such, she is seen as an object of deceit and repulsion, the personification of feminism as a threat to patriarchal norms. For some feminists, she is a hero for precisely the same reasons. For many women of color, on the other hand, Schumer breezily assumes that her version of feminism is inclusive and

---

1. I am building on the argument advanced in an earlier article I cowrote with Viveca Greene ("Asking for It: Rape Myths, Satire, and Feminist Lacunae," *Signs: Journal of Women in Culture and Society*, vol. 45, no. 2, 2020). That article is more specifically about feminist satire of sexual violence but also contains the assertion that Schumer can be seen as a stand-in for mainstream white feminism (in all its strengths and flaws). I remain indebted to Dr. Greene for helping to generate this idea.

welcoming while long remaining blind to her own forms of privilege and to the ways her comedy could be further entrenching racist assumptions. To this constituency, Schumer is representative of white feminism's history as myopic and racist. How spectators react to her comedy, then, is overlaid by their relationship to mainstream white feminism. Schumer, of course, did not nominate herself as feminism's popular culture representative, but once put in that position, it was inevitable that she would become the object of loathing for many, both because of the virulence of popular misogyny as well as the feminist movement's own internal contradictions.

Industry Shifts

Though Schumer has participated in a variety of forms of comedy, her reputation was cemented with her sketch program *Inside Amy Schumer*. Sketch comedy is a form that can arguably be traced as far back as commedia dell'arte. In the United States, its beginnings were in the world of vaudeville. When television came on the scene, sketch comedy became one of the many forms in rotation on variety programs (such as *The Colgate Comedy Hour, Rowan and Martin's Laugh In*, and *The Smothers Brothers Comedy Hour*). But it is the long-running program *Saturday Night Live* (*SNL*) that truly institutionalized the form in American television. *SNL*'s popularity did much to raise the profile of sketch comedy. It also opened doors for many comedians attempting to gain recognition, including many women. However, at the beginnings of the program, there was a notorious "climate of institutionalized sexism" (Marx 66). As Nick Marx puts it, "the show's men subjected women writers, performers, and producers early on to a range of maltreatment. The generally hostile environment toward women meant that screen time for them was less meaningful and their comedic voices factored into the program less than those of men" (66). Accounts from individual women involved in the show vary as to whether they were able to navigate the culture of that workplace or not, but in Yael Kohen's oral history of women in comedy, several of the early *SNL* players report that cast members such as John Belushi and Al Franken routinely announced that women were not funny or refused to perform in sketches written by female writers (Kohen 104).

The culture of *SNL* has evolved somewhat over the years and with different cast members. Tina Fey's tenure at the show was particularly significant for shifting some of its dynamics. She was hired as a writer for the program in 1997, becoming head writer a couple years later and a featured performer shortly thereafter. While she wrote all sorts of material, she did frequently bring a more feminist outlook to her comedy than had been common on the program previously. This dynamic increased with the subsequent addition of Amy Poehler in 2001, particularly when the two performers began coanchoring the Weekend Update segment. Both have gone on to have extremely successful comedy careers after leaving *SNL*, though as Marx explains of Fey, "her success is still commonly framed around the aspirational idea of a woman making it in a comedy world dominated by men. Although such discourses can indeed be empowering, they obfuscate the underlying, assumed norm—that sketch comedy is and should be predominantly masculine and that success by a woman is inherently transgressive" (91). Nevertheless, the fact that they both were such bankable stars (headlining their own television programs and starring in films) made it more plausible for someone like Amy Schumer to be given her own sketch platform by Comedy Central in 2013. How various constituencies would react to Schumer's comedy, though, is another story.

Schumer's Feminist Comedy

Schumer's comedic style combines vulgarity with often trenchant social commentary. She frequently portrays a somewhat vapid or vain character, but that viewpoint is typically superseded by the intelligence behind her jokes. On *IAS* in particular, Schumer is most observant when taking on the cultural contradictions and cruelties around gender norms, frequently skewering both the larger culture and the conflicted and often self-defeating individuals the culture produces. As Taylor Nygaard observes, Schumer's milieu is most certainly the postfeminist landscape around her, but while postfeminism implicitly denies the necessity for feminism, "*IAS* uses parody and satire not as a means to deflect or preempt feminist critique, but rather to inspire a sustained interrogation of postfeminist discourse as a dominant sensibility" (65). Indeed, many of the sketches highlight the mixed messages of a postfeminist culture. For instance, one sketch is presented as a faux music video in which a peppy boy band begins by crooning to Schumer "girl you don't need makeup; you're perfect when you wake up" and imploring her to wipe it all off. However, when she actually does, the horrified boys amend the song to tell her that she definitely needs to put it back on, likening her face to the floor that time they tried to rip up shag carpeting expecting there to be hardwood underneath but finding only dirty linoleum ("Cool with It"). Her

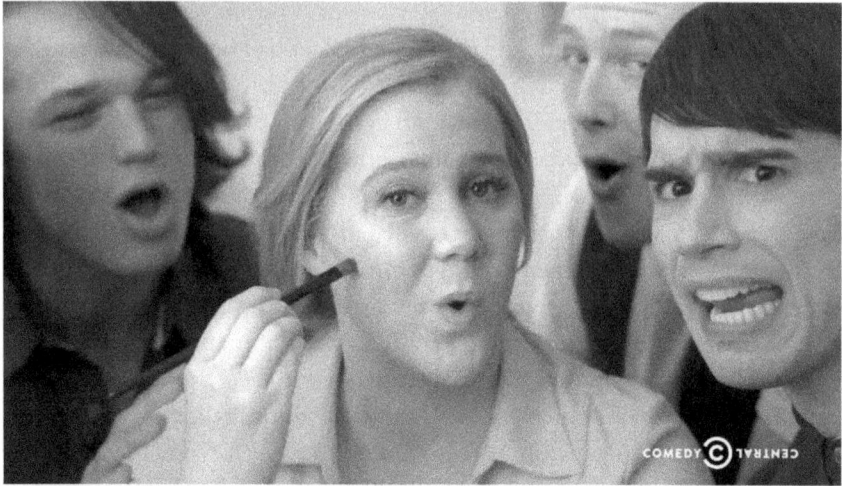

Figure 3.1. Amy Schumer on her sketch program *Inside Amy Schumer*, pictured with a boy band horrified by the bare face she reveals under her makeup.

female characters are often trying and failing to live up to schizophrenic social messages and expectations.

Particularly when she was first starting out, much was made of Schumer's presumed ability to straddle demographics by playing up her femininity and sex appeal while simultaneously critiquing the construction of both. *Inside Amy Schumer* ran on Comedy Central, a network with a famously male-heavy audience, and her show pulled in respectable numbers. At the start of the program's second season, Willa Paskin of *Slate* magazine lauded the program's "sneaky feminism," arguing that "Schumer hides her intellect in artifice and lip gloss—that's how she performs femininity. By wrapping her ideas in a ditzy, sexy, slutty, self-hating shtick, her message goes down easy—and only then, like the alien, sticks its opinionated teeth in you." She explains that "Schumer's self-presentation, along with the peppering in of low-brow dirty jokes and sketches in which she plays the vapid asshole, are extremely shrewd: Amy Schumer doesn't 'seem' like a feminist who can't take a joke. On *Inside Amy Schumer*, she's the feminist who makes them."

While Paskin sees a tactical victory in Schumer offering feminist critique for a dude-heavy audience, Nick Marx argues that the explicit feminism on the program itself was effectively undercut by the way in which Comedy Central chose to market it (137). His larger argument is about the economic power surrounding sketch comedy (the nuts and bolts of its production and distribution) inevitably limiting the potentially empowering cultural meanings of the sketch comedy genre, pointing to Comedy Central attempting to tout its many seemingly contentious comedies helmed by a diverse stable of talent while ultimately still tethering all the programs to the tastes of straight white men. In the case of *IAS*, that involved using advertising images of Schumer that played up her heterosexual attractiveness. Nygaard, however, attempts to recuperate the program's feminist resonance by noting that though the show actually had quite tepid viewing numbers on television in its third (and most unmistakably feminist) season, it had an enormous number of online viewers for individual sketches (68). In other words, those who appreciated the feminist critique were able to find it, with or without Comedy Central. I would argue that it clearly demonstrates a shift in who was seeking out the show and how they were interacting with it, likely indicating that the much-lauded balance between appealing to the bro audience and asserting a feminist politics was an unsustainable one. I would point out that it is right about the same moment that there was a clearly developing fracturing audience response to Schumer as a performer. On the one hand, she won a Peabody award in 2014, signaling that her show was being taken seriously for its critique, and as Nygaard notes, her most biting feminist sketches were concurrently the ones that were being most actively shared on social media. On the other hand, it is at roughly the same moment that Schumer starts to become a clear target for that feminism, angrily dismissed by many who did not appreciate her perspective and actively hounded by those who feel most threatened by it.

Of course, to point to all of Schumer's comedy as flawlessly feminist would be an overstatement. Like most comedy, her work is not univocal, particularly as it is translated across multiple forms with different genre imperatives and logics (stand-up, sketch, and Hollywood film) and through the minds of many individual contributing writers. And as with most comedy, sometimes the jokes simply do not land. Further, comedy that pokes fun of entrenched norms and stereotypes always runs the risk of simply reinforcing those stereotypes. Putting aside Schumer's issues around race for the moment, her work on gender alone can at times slide so heavily into self-deprecation that it can seem to sanction some of the most pernicious gender stereotypes. Her repeated, baroquely embellished riffs on her vagina, for instance, can signify in a number of different ways. As Maggie Hennefeld explains, "This is at least partly why Schumer's grotesque bodily and sexual humor sometimes becomes repetitively gimmicky and borderline misogynistic—especially in her stand-up performances, late night interviews, and various other media appearances" (98). But that is also because her humor is directed both at larger systemic issues as well as the way in which individuals contort themselves in response. As Hennefeld puts it, "there exist two key modes of laugher on *Inside Amy Schumer*: aggressive, derisive laughter at the absurdities of structural sexism, and a destabilizing, self-flagellating laughter at the equally oppressive norms of cosmopolitan femininity" (99). The show does not shy away from depicting the ways in which women can be complicit in shoring up some of the most pernicious aspects of patriarchy.

There are undeniably a slew of hard-hitting sketches from *IAS* that shrewdly highlight the cruelties of twenty-first-century sexism. Many of the most pithy or incisive have found broad circulation, for instance, a sketch from the show's third season featuring appearances by several famous guest actresses: Tina Fey, Patricia Arquette, and Julia Louis-Dreyfuss. In the sketch, Schumer is out for a run in a bucolic field when she stumbles across the three performers settled around a beautifully laid-out feast. A star-struck Schumer eagerly joins the women and inquires if they are celebrating a birthday. Fey informs her that they are instead celebrating Louis-Dreyfuss's "last fuckable day." When a confused Schumer asks what that is, they elaborate that "in every actress's life, the media decides when you finally reach the point when you are not believably fuckable anymore" ("Last F…able Day"). They explain that there are plenty of signs when you have reached the threshold—for instance, when Sally Field played Tom Hanks's love interest but then was cast as his mother just a short time later or when they start remaking your movies with younger, more "fuckable" actresses. Schumer naively asks who tells men when it is their last fuckable day, and the three laugh heartily, informing her that men remain fuckable forever. At one point in the sketch, Fey mentions to everyone that actor Bruce Willis is dating someone twenty-four years younger than him who is an actual baby lamb, tipping the sketch toward the absurd. This segment was a popular one, as it succinctly encapsulates the double standard around beauty ideals, particularly for women in the public eye. Another widely lauded sketch (which was actually an entire episode long) took on similar themes, this time structured as a parody of the movie *Twelve Angry Men*. Only, in this version, the men around the table are impassionedly debating whether or not Schumer herself is hot enough to be on television. Guest actor Jeff Goldblum, who plays the foreman of the jury, explains in the segment, "if we decide that she is not bang-able, then she is going to lose her television show, or be put to immediate death.... Or both. To be honest, I zoned out during that part" ("12 Angry Men Inside Amy Schumer"). The episode, in fact, repeats a number of the insults routinely lobbed at Schumer online about her appearance (including those mentioned at the start of this chapter), clearly demonstrating both how hurtful they are and how absurd the logic is that would judge the quality of her program based on subjective opinions about her appearance.

Other sketches take on darker material, including a handful explicitly about sexual assault and rape culture (also discussed at length in Greene and Day). For example, one takes the form of a parody of the television program *Friday Night Lights*, in which the new coach of the small-town high school football team lays down new rules, including "no raping," shocking and befuddling the players. As they struggle to understand the rule and test its loopholes, they repeat (in absurdly exaggerated fashion) nearly every rape myth in existence. Though the earnest coach grows ever more exasperated over the players' wish to skirt the rule, in his final, midgame inspirational speech, he himself unwittingly reinforces rape culture, yelling that football is not about rape, it is "about violently dominating anyone that stands between you and what you want. You got to get yourself into the mindset that you are gods! And you are entitled to this! That other team? They ain't just going to lay down and give it to you! You got to go out there and take it" ("Last F... able Day"). The sketch draws attention to the self-reinforcing links between sports culture and rape culture while highlighting the variety of rape myths used to excuse sexual violence or blame the victim, sometimes perpetuated by women themselves (such as two elderly neighbors of the coach who spit at his feet while out for their power walk).

Antifeminist Backlash

The clearly pointed feminist sketches, such as those previously described, are the ones that are both routinely circulated by fans online and that receive the most vitriol by antifans online. For example, in the comments section under the *Football Town Nights* sketch on YouTube, while there are enthusiastic commenters who praise the sketch or appreciatively repeat some of the funnier lines, there are skeins of extremely negative comments that attack both Schumer and the sketch. Some take issue with the premise or the implications of the satire, complaining that the segment unfairly implies that all men are rapists or taking umbrage with the very concept of rape culture that, many assert, "feminazis" have been pushing. For instance, one post begins, "The Western world does not live in a 'Rape Culture.' Enough of this nonsense. Disagree? Fuck you. Fuck off." Many of the commenters complain that the skit demonstrates a double standard, as men are criticized for telling rape jokes, so why should women be allowed to do so? Other comments simply announce that Schumer is some combination of not funny, ugly, or fat. As one commenter puts it, "this is shit!! Who would rape miss piggy anyway?"

While it might seem like a capitulation to misogyny to explicitly discuss Schumer's relative beauty here, I think it is worth noting that by any real-world standard, she would be considered conventionally attractive. Particularly when she first began attracting attention, she was a young, white, blonde woman who routinely played up her femininity in her style of dress. Over the years, her weight has fluctuated somewhat, much of the time within the range of what would be considered relatively thin/healthy for the average woman but often heavier than most Hollywood actresses, even as Schumer was posing for a variety of magazine shoots. Her seeming confidence about her appearance and refusal to attempt to starve her body into submission as a woman in the public eye seems to be a particular source of upset for a lot of male onlookers. A striking number of commenters on any article or video involving Schumer call her fat or ugly (usually in much more descriptive terms). The seeming anger around Schumer's appearance is likely not helped by the fact that, as discussed, during *IAS*'s run, Comedy Central was routinely playing up her sexuality in its advertisements for the show, clearly incensing many who don't see her as sufficiently beautiful. Returning to Linda Mizejewski's thesis that female performers have historically been allowed to be either pretty or funny but not both, Schumer's attempt to have it all elicits hatred from many, along with a desire to punish the comedian. Many commenters also build their insults around the presumption that she is sexually promiscuous, though one would think that line of attack wouldn't be all that satisfying, as Schumer herself constructed her bad-girl persona around similar ideas, opening a stand-up segment in the first episode of *IAS* with the declaration that she is "sluttier than the average bear" ("Bad Decisions").

The insults lobbed at Schumer are clearly not anomalous; rather, they are entirely consistent with dominant patterns of what Karla Mantilla dubs "gender trolling," the specific tactics that members of the manosphere use when attacking publicly vocal women. As Mantilla details, "women are especially attacked for being not sexually attractive enough to men. . . . for being, in the eye of the gendertroll, fat, 'ugly,' old, or a 'dyke.' Women are criticized for being too sexual (they are whores or sluts), or they are disparaged for having female body parts, which are used as insults (they are 'cunts' or their genitalia are especially disparaged)" (41). Often these comments lead to a judgment as to the woman's "rape-ability or the degree to which she deserves to be raped" (41). All are intended to shame a woman and to chase her out of the public sphere. As Mantilla explains, the thing that victims of gender trolling all have in common is that they are women publicly expressing their opinion about something. Though that opinion can be about almost anything, "having opinions affirmatively in favor of any aspect of women's rights seems to incur the most attention of the harassers. . . . And it is often worse if she advocates for women's self-respect, equal representation, or self-determination, however mildly and to however limited an audience" (37). While Schumer's political beliefs may have been more unclear when she first began doing stand-up, as her fame increased and her sketch program provided her with a more expansive platform, her feminist sympathies became much harder to miss. Perhaps predictably, then, as Mantilla explains, "groups of men from various sites on the Internet find out that a woman has taken such a stand, often going out of their way to search out such assertiveness on the part of women, and then rally their too-numerous troops to wage an all-out campaign to seek retribution on the targeted women in whatever ways they can" (37).

In Schumer's case, the trolls did get organized en masse, launching campaigns to actively trash her ratings and reviews, first for her book in 2016 and then for her Netflix stand-up set *The Leather Special* in 2017 (Wright), in a way reminiscent of the anti-*Ghostbusters* attacks. The goal in such campaigns is to flood online rating systems with one-star reviews so that the average score for the book, or video, or whatnot is incredibly low (even if other individuals have given it a high rating), theoretically decreasing subsequent interest in the product. Indeed some (angrily) intuited a connection between Schumer's *Leather Special* ratings and Netflix's decision a couple weeks after its release to change their user-generated ratings system (Hashmi), though Netflix denied the link. In addition, there have been a number of online commentators who have worked hard to circulate the charge that Schumer has stolen jokes from other comics. The accusation was initially launched by three other female comics who accused Schumer of using jokes that were similar to their own. The three subsequently retracted their accusation, stating that it could have been a case of parallel thinking (Abad-Santos "Amy Schumer's"), but a number of antifans latched on to the charges and added examples of additional jokes in her oeuvre that they thought were similar to those of other comics, creating compilations on YouTube to fan the flames, trying to spread the word that Schumer is a joke stealer. While it is extremely difficult to adjudicate whether a comic has intentionally stolen a concept from another comic, many famous comedians have had similar accusations directed at them. However, few have been hounded about it to quite the same degree. Marc Maron, who hosts the popular comedy podcast *WTF*, spent some time addressing the accusations against Schumer on his program, as he had taken umbrage with being included in an online compilation as one of the comedians she had supposedly robbed. Maron first attempted to debunk each of the individual charges against Schumer and then went on to diagnose the controversy as existing solely due to misogyny. He explains that he has seen the pattern before, as whenever he has a woman on his show, the comments section online is inevitably riddled by ugly, violent taunts and insults. He argues, "this has nothing to do with justice. This is about annihilating a woman . . . they put a lot of work into it—to the point where they manipulated my words to suit their agenda and get that through" (Abad-Santos "Marc Maron"). Maron explicitly links attitudes toward Schumer as a comic to her identity as a woman.

Beyond simply being a female entertainer, though, Schumer seems to be the recipient of hatred that is especially white hot. Aside from the targeted campaigns, the comments about Schumer online in practically every venue (beneath YouTube clips, under articles about her, etc.) are both plentiful and strikingly vitriolic. On Urban Dictionary, the many definitions listed under the name "Amy Schumer" include "literally the worst comedian to ever exist" and "a Fat, Ugly, and Unfunny Comedian who has an Obsession with making Jokes about her vagina. Anyone who enjoys watching Amy Schumers Comedy Deserve to Die a Slow Painful Death. Literally nobody finds her funny [*sic*]." When one scans the comments below the work of other female comedians with a comparatively similar style, it is not uncommon to see compliments given to the other comic as an opportunity to disparage Schumer in comparison. For instance, in the case of Ali Wong, a comedian also known for her explicit, bawdy humor, comments under compilations of her jokes on YouTube include a number along the lines of "Amy Schumer wished she was half as funny as Ali Wong," followed by rejoinders such as "I'm gonna report you for making me read her name without warning." It is hard to tell if these types of comments on unrelated texts and performances are part of the coordinated effort to tarnish Schumer's reputation, but it seems more likely that those organized campaigns have resulted in a great deal of genuine loathing that is happily self-perpetuating.

Writing on antifandom, Jonathan Gray describes "bad objects" that somehow become the focus of widespread cultural scorn. As an example, he gives pop singer Miley Cyrus, who became a "lightening rod for dislike within popular culture" (29) in the fall of 2013. He muses that while some might have been predisposed to hate her due to a gendered disdain of pop icons, or an aversion to her style of music, or disapproval over her behavior, it is most likely that these reasons and many more intersected "and in doing so strengthened the resolve of any one 'entryway' to the Bad Object anti-fandom. If one hates pop music, therefore, one has any number of options of figures and bands to dislike, but when Cyrus is so widely reviled by others for other reasons, it simply becomes easier to nominate her the representative of pop music and to focus one's dislike in her direction" (29). In Schumer's case, she has become the representative of all the imagined dangers of feminism. Thus, even those who might not associate themselves with the manosphere or who wouldn't normally actively target outspoken women but who perhaps have some reservations about feminism can bond with other men online by lobbing insults at Amy Schumer.

Racial Blind Spots

Despite the unmistakable misogyny directed at Schumer, feelings about her as a comedian do not divide up neatly around either gendered or political lines. There is also a great deal of dislike for her on the political left, often from women, though for very different reasons than those given by the bros. In this case, she has come under intense criticism for some of her material involving race. Particularly early in her career, Schumer had a number of jokes/moments that were questioned for their racial insensitivity, which she followed up with assertions that her feminism was inclusive of all women and that her comedy could not possibly be problematic. However, these statements were not accompanied by any noticeable effort to adjust how she approached race as a comic. Instead, Schumer largely repeated many of the mistakes that have been made historically by white feminists who have assumed that their brand of feminism is automatically representative of all women.

As Schumer exploded into popular visibility in 2015, the many celebrity profiles and complimentary articles about her smart gender politics were followed by several critiques of her racial politics. These articles turned a spotlight on some of Schumer's earlier stand-up routines as well as her turn hosting the MTV music awards. For instance, in an otherwise quite complimentary column about Schumer in *The Guardian*, Monica Heisey notes that "for such a keen observer of social norms and an effective satirist of the ways gender is complicated by them, Schumer has a shockingly large blind spot around race," going on to explain that her early stand-up included throwaway lines like "nothing works 100 percent of the time, except Mexicans" and "I used to date Hispanic guys, but now I prefer consensual." Without explicitly mentioning Heisey by name, Schumer responded defensively to this criticism on Twitter shortly after the article had come out. She writes:

> I am a comic. I am so glad more people are laughing at me and with me all
> of a sudden. I will joke about things you like and I will joke about things
> you aren't comfortable with. And that's ok. Stick with me and trust I am
> joking. I go in and out of playing an irreverent idiot. That includes making
> dumb jokes involving race. I enjoy playing the girl who time to time says
> that dumbest thing possible and playing with race is a thing we are not
> supposed to do, which is what makes it so fun for comics. You can call it
> a "blind spot for racism" or "lazy" but you are wrong. It is a joke and it is
> funny. I know that because people laugh at it. . . .

Schumer is essentially giving two reasons why she does not believe that her comedy is ever problematic. One is that she is only joking, and so the jokes couldn't possibly be racist, pointing to the laughter of her audience as a barometer for whether she is succeeding. This is specious logic, which needs some unpacking. The other reason, given when she references the character she plays onstage, is that the joke is definitely on her character for being a dumb racist rather than on the victims of racism. This is the more defensible reasoning, and we will explore it first.

Indeed, as discussed earlier, Schumer as writer/comedian often stands several steps removed from the characters she plays, who we are invited to judge. As Emily Nussbaum puts it, the "grotty, chaotic persona that Schumer has developed" allows her "to poke just as hard at young single women, in their blinkered vanity, as she does at the toxic messages that surround them" ("Little Tramp"). It is a form of comedy that Nygaard refers to as a type of "stiob," a Russian tradition of humor in which statements are presented as if they were earnest, though they are meant to be read ironically, while the mimicry is often so precise that it can be difficult to tell if it is to be interpreted as sincere or as subtle ridicule. The danger of such humor is that it "risks looking so like what it critiques that it reinforces stereotypes" (63). It is not a stretch to say that Schumer has long played with all facets of her entitled white girl character. Sometimes, as discussed, her portrayals veer a little too closely into the territory of misogynist stereotypes, though when she is at her best, the wit of the writing usually interrogates those stereotypes. However, as Dustin Bradley Goltz notes, "Schumer's performative doing of femininity and disruption of sexism is particularly enabled in her body, in a manner that her doing of racism through her white feminine body . . . is limited and discursively directed" (277). In other words, she is adept at using her body as an attractive, ciswoman to complicate and unpack the messages around gender but certainly cannot do the same for the cultural messages around race. If anything, it can read as another white woman flippantly repeating racial stereotypes, even if that is not the intention. To make matters worse, it can be difficult to separate the ironic version of Schumer from the one who shows up in interviews and other public venues. One of the jokes that Heisey singled out in her article was not from Schumer's stand-up but from her patter while hosting the MTV music awards in 2015 in which she off-handedly referred to all Latinas as "crazy." There was certainly no follow up to the comment that would have directed the joke back at Schumer. So, while Schumer is telling the truth that she often intentionally plays a clueless or ill-informed character, she also would have to do more work for the comments that character (or her own public persona) makes about race to be successfully inverted or interrogated.

Her other knee-jerk response, that she is just being funny and experimenting with edgy jokes, is an extremely common one, but it is still remarkably naive. There is an incredibly long history of humor being used to reinforce social boundaries and hierarchies. Historically, when jokes are told by members of the majority about minority groups, the minority groups do not find themselves flattered. Beginning with blackface minstrelsy, there is a shameful history in the United States in particular of using ethnic/racial humor to shore up the superiority of the majority and justify the debasement of minorities. As such, to maintain that an audience's laughter is enough to ascertain whether a joke has succeeded, and is thus defensible as a joke, is to entirely ignore systemic injustice and power. Schumer assumes that her intentions should be the guide to how her jokes are interpreted: because she is not intending to be racist, the jokes cannot actually have that effect. Rául Pérez, who conducted an ethnography of a stand-up comedy school, describes white comics being coached into using self-deprecation, distancing, and denial techniques to make an audience comfortable with them then playing with stereotypes of racial others. Audiences would be made comfortable with the jokes if they first felt assured that the comic could him- or herself take a joke, or if they had somehow signaled that they were themselves aware of (and thus distant from) racism. But, as he explains (citing J. J. Feagin), "racism is not solely a question of individual prejudice, but of actors legitimizing racial hierarchies, reinforcing racial power structures and reproducing racial ideologies" (Pérez 499).

Another term that has been used informally to discuss these kinds of jokes is *hipster racism*. In a *Guardian* article, Rachel Dubrofsky is quoted pithily defining the concept as being the "domain of white, often progressive people who think they are hip to racism, which they mistakenly believe gives them permission to say and do racist things without actually being racist" (Mahdawi), usually because they are making use of irony. The term helpfully indicates that intention is largely irrelevant when it comes to the continued perpetuation of racist ideas. And, as Pérez explains, the point "is not only that peripheral 'genuine racists' might be emboldened through the mainstreaming of racist comedy, but that the unique and frequently unchallenged (re)production of racism through humor more generally fits within the larger logic of a shifting racial discourse in public" (499), which always obscures itself by presenting as something other than racism. In the case of Schumer's initial response to being criticized for her race-based jokes, the most problematic element is her unwillingness to entertain the idea that they might be hurtful and her assumption that humor automatically provides a shield from critique. She further asserts, "Trust me. I am not racist. I am a devout feminist and lover of all people. My fight is for all people to be treated equally." Here she equates feminism with antiracism, without demonstrating how she might be advancing an intersectional brand of feminism that would respond to the needs of a diverse array of women.

In her response, Schumer also mentions that she had avoided any jokes involving race for the previous two years (implying that she will carry on doing so). And for the most part, that is true; however, she has continued to display tone-deaf instincts in some of the creative choices in subsequent material. For instance, in 2017, Schumer starred (with Goldie Hawn) in a film called *Snatched* about a mother and daughter who go on a vacation to Ecuador but are promptly abducted and must outwit their captors. It is styled as a sort of screwball dark comedy involving broad characters all around, but the film leans heavily on stereotypes of Latin American men as violent gangsters to make its premise believable while telling another archetypal tale about white women in peril. According to Michelle Colpean and Meg Tully, the film attempts to have it all by engaging in "weak reflexivity," which they explain "is a form of weak intersectionality that allows white feminist comedians to joke about their whiteness without critically examining it, ultimately reproducing dominant racial ideologies rather than working to dismantle them" (162). They argue that the film occasionally gestures to the main characters' whiteness for laughs, often as a way of explaining their ignorance, but it ultimately functions as "a convenient excuse or a silly misunderstanding rather than a powerful force that drives systemic injustice" (170). The jokes then are used to "capitalize on some level of awareness" but stop well short of "alienating their mostly white audiences with any significant interrogation of whiteness" (171).

Granted, it should be acknowledged that Schumer neither wrote nor directed the film, so she certainly did not have sole creative control over its narrative. However, she did throw her star power behind it. And it is fairly consistent with some of her other work. In addition, while she, Hawn, and other costars were filming *Snatched*, they also took the time to film a music video based on Beyoncé's song "Formation" (from her *Lemonade* album) that was received badly by a large number of viewers. Beyoncé's own video had been produced (and embraced by fans) as a proud tribute to Black womanhood, making an explicitly political statement by referencing post–Hurricane Katrina Louisiana as well as the Black Lives Matter movement and ultimately calling for Black female solidarity. When Schumer's version was released, most assumed that the video was intended as a parody, though Schumer later insisted that it was a tribute. And, indeed, there is nothing in her video that seems to be explicitly poking fun of the original; however, her decision to echo or repurpose the beloved original does seem remarkably tone-deaf, and her response to the backlash was worse.

Her first official comment after the release was an Instagram post that read, "You know you that bitch when you cause all this conversation. Thanks for the exclusive release Tidal! We had so much fun making this tribute. All love and women inspiring each other. #strongertogether," underneath a photo of her lounging in her underwear. When the criticism continued, she wrote a longer article, explaining again that the video had been intended as an homage, as she and the rest of the cast of *Snatched* had been obsessed with Beyoncé's song, listening to it repeatedly while simultaneously paying rapt attention to Hillary Clinton's then campaign for the presidency. She goes on: "I love how in the lyrics of 'Formation' Beyoncé is telling us to get in formation. . . . I am of course horrified and sickened by the events that are addressed throughout that video and didn't see this as minimizing that and still don't. It was a way to celebrate bringing us all together. To fight for what we all want. And to do it together" (Schumer "Information"). She further explains that her mission is "to continue to work as hard as I can to empower women and make them laugh and feel better and I won't let anything stop me." Schumer seems to miss the fact that Beyoncé was speaking to Black women about their experiences in particular. She also assumes that her version of feminism encompasses the concerns of all women, unwittingly reproducing the historical blindness of white feminism in the United States, which has long struggled to address the fact that gender is experienced differently across boundaries of race, class, sexuality, and abilities, instead presuming that the experiences of middle-class white women are universal. As George Yancy puts it, "whiteness, within the feminist movement, has assumed a position of absolute authority, speaking from a center which marginalizes non-white voices" (158). For many, Schumer's calls for unity were part of that larger insidious pattern. As a writer for the *Daily Beast* explains, "for centuries, women of color have often felt as though their invitation to the big feminist party has gotten lost in the mail. That's why, when Amy Schumer tries to say that Lemonade is for every woman, black Twitter throws its own party" (Zimmerman). Here she is referencing the hashtag that began trending in the days after Schumer released her video: #AmySchumerGottaGoParty.

For many, when they look at Schumer, they see her career success "as a straight, white, cis-gender, able-bodied, conventionally pretty woman as evidence of the limited version of feminism that attains mainstream mediated visibility" (Nygaard 69). Like the majority of successful performers, Schumer has benefited from her whiteness. But she also rarely acknowledges or interrogates that benefit. Instead, she often seems rather blind to it and defensive about any reminders, while self-congratulatory about her politics. As Colpean and Tully argue of both Schumer and Tina Fey (another popular white feminist comedian who has been similarly accused of racial insensitivity), "their consistent refusals to critically examine their whiteness reinforce white feminism's privileging of gender over other identity markers. Labeling whiteness but retreating from meaningful engagement with race leaves the burden of racial justice to those in the most precarious positions" (177). The hurt, of course, is not simply about Schumer or Fey, but about a much longer history. Thus, while some feminist fans thrill to the fact that voices like Schumer's and Fey's are finally being heard within popular culture, others remain frustrated that "largely positive mass media reviews reinforce this brand of white feminism as a celebrated form of progress rather than a complicated reflection of contemporary fractures" (Colpean and Tully 174). Ultimately, Schumer's success is read as symbolic by a variety of different onlookers with a variety of different perspectives.

It is worth noting that Schumer and Fey consider themselves to be both antiracist and politically progressive. But they have not demonstrated a lot of introspection or willingness to learn when faced with criticism on their material when it comes to race, instead assuming that their progressive intentions are what count most. Due to the double-voiced nature of irony, satire about racial injustice and stereotypes (as well as satire about sexual inequality, sexual orientation, etc.) is always dangerous, running the risk of confirming stereotypes even as it seeks to dismantle them. What complicates things for a performer like Amy Schumer is that her response to criticism has been remarkably similar in the face of attacks from the alt-right and to pushback for racial insensitivity (at least initially), but that response reads exceedingly differently in the two circumstances. When it comes to the antifeminist assaults, Schumer has been lauded for her unapologetic self-confidence and unwillingness to be cowed. When she cuttingly (but humorously) shut down a sexist interviewer, magazine headlines crowed about her triumph (Vagianos). And as trolls attempted to make insults about her appearance into an art form, she deconstructed their logic and viciousness in her comedy. In other words, her response has been to not back down. That has been precisely the wrong response to criticism about the messages she is sending on race, but it appears to have again been her first instinct. After repeated clapback and a huge number of critical blog posts and articles, Schumer has become more contrite, acknowledging that she has made mistakes.

The criticism she has received about her treatment of race is undoubtedly justified, though, confusingly, as a writer for the *New Yorker* puts it, "the fair critiques have inadvertently sanctioned plain and simple misogyny, and an unfocussed loathing of her brand of vulgar irreverence" (St. Felix). For example, in the deluge of comments on her initial Twitter post and photo responding to criticism about the "Formation" video, some of the most frequent comments, as usual, are about her looking like a whale or about the posters wanting to vomit from seeing her picture. In many of the more mainstream forums, it all blends into an undefined hatred of her as an individual. As is the case with most celebrities, who cannot possibly be personal friends with the majority of viewers, what both fans and antifans have access to is the persona, a persona who very easily becomes a symbol. In Schumer's case, I believe that she has become symbolic of white feminism. Whether she is the most radical of feminists or the most egregious of racists matters fairly little, as she has become a stand-in. As such, when we examine reactions to Schumer, we can see both the power structures contemporary popular feminism threatens and the ones it often unwittingly upholds.

The Popular-Cultural Face of White Feminism

In Sarah Banet-Weiser's account (explored in greater detail in previous chapters), though misogyny has been around for a very long time, its current iteration as "popular misogyny" exists precisely because popular feminism has itself become visible. As she explains, the widespread public shaming of women (including the shaming of bodies, sexual practices, and personal histories) "has become a normative tool for expressing an imagined injustice. This injustice can be specific and personal, such as a girlfriend breaking up with a man, or more diffused, such as the affront apparently felt when a woman takes up space in what was previously a masculine realm, either through voice, body, or political sentiment" (85). Someone like Schumer must be particularly enraging for popular misogynists as she seems unwilling to be cowed. She continues to speak forthrightly about gendered inequality, continues to find success in the male-dominated field of comedy (naughty, sometimes explicit comedy at that), and continues to showcase her body even when it is met with opprobrium. She is a target of popular misogyny who has thumbed her nose at the intimidation. Just as she invites loathing by those who see feminism as a threat then, her career success and self-confidence have been widely interpreted as a significant win for popular feminist visibility.

At the same time, however, Schumer's celebrity is also a stark reminder of who is more likely to ascend to those heights. As Banet-Weiser puts it, much of the time, "the popular feminism that is most visible is that which is white, middle-class, cis-gendered, and heterosexual" (13). Who is visible in popular feminism is also fairly representative of who is in positions of leadership within feminist organizations. As Patricia Hill Collins explained in 2006, "more than thirty years after the feminist movement encountered charges of racism and elitism, the executive directors of women's organizations and their senior staffs are still overwhelmingly White" (174). It is little wonder then that mainstream (white) feminism has largely continued to pursue an agenda that universalizes the experience of white, middle-class women. Worse, that agenda has historically often worked against women of color. Relatedly, Taigi Smith explains, second-wave feminism focused to a great degree on liberating middle-class women from housework and childcare, but that was possible only because the work could be relegated to women of color. As she puts it, the movement "largely liberated white women at the economic and social expense of women of color" (62).

When white feminists urge all women to put aside their differences and work for the cause as one, without acknowledging any of this history, it can understandably rankle women of color. While for some whites, it may seem like a laudable goal to strive for "colorblindness," in moving ahead together while attempting not to notice race, as Barbara Tomlinson explains, "colorblindness is not a social theory, a moral imperative, or a route to racial equality but rather a way to hide, excuse, justify, and protect the unfair gains and unjust enrichments of centuries of expressly racist practices and policies" (175). To assume that race is irrelevant in many situations is arguably a particularly insidious form of white privilege. Collins points out that many of us are used to racializing explanations for social ills such as poverty or crime (i.e., understanding that there might be a structural component), but, she explains, most white people fail to apply this same logic to their own situation of privilege. Rather, "whites routinely attribute their own success not to unfair advantage emanating from their group classification as Whites in a racial formulation that privileges Whiteness, but to their individual attributes, such as ability, talent, motivation, self-discipline, and hard work" (179). Not being aware of one's privilege works, of course, to help shore up the system from which one benefits. The strains of mainstream (white) feminism that have resisted intersectional analysis have undoubtedly worked to prop up existing systems of power that disadvantage minorities (of race, class, sexuality, and ability).

Schumer's self-description as a feminist combined with her often flippant treatment of race, as well as her reluctance to acknowledge her own privilege, makes her an easy, high-profile representative of the ills of white feminism. In the discourse around her work, we can see all of the fault lines around mainstream feminism mapped in stark relief: a social justice movement that is, in many ways, seen as threatening to the status quo, while it is also only belatedly beginning to grapple with its blind investment in other harmful structures of power.

I want to be clear that the criticism around Schumer's insensitivity and lack of self-reflection on race is often warranted. However, it is also worth noting that she receives an outsize amount of attention given the hordes of white performers/politicians/corporate spokespeople/others in the public eye who have arguably as little or less understanding of racial privilege. Being held up as the face of mainstream white feminism becomes a game that Schumer is ultimately doomed to lose no matter how she calibrates her comedy, as both the political Left and Right will always find her inadequate. As we have explored, feminist performers, particularly feminist comedians, seem to attract both positive and negative projections far more than others.

At the height of Schumer's rise in popularity in 2015, television critic Emily Nussbaum somewhat predicted what would come next. She explained that there was a risk to Schumer's ascent, warning, "now comes the hype, the lash and the backlash and the backlash to the backlash, the hero worship and the red-hot fury—no pressure, Amy Schumer! It's happened again and again to the new wave of female TV creators, the Tinas and Mindys and Lenas, whose fans want role models as well as artists—a demand that many female comics embrace but that's rarely required of men" ("Little Tramp"). Granted, what remains unsaid in Nussbaum's summation is that two of the three other comic performers/writers that she names (Tina Fey and Lena Dunham) have also been justifiably accused of having similar blind spots around race. They are both also white feminists who have struggled to grapple with white privilege, again offering a telling indication of which female performers have been the ones to achieve career success. But the fact also remains that the red-hot fury, from all corners, like the adulation, the moral opprobrium, and the fascination, seems to be disproportionately lavished on the feminist comedians of all types. Feminism and feminist comedy are the contested concepts on which onlookers project their own fears and desires. Time and again, feminist comedians become the bellwether of the various battle lines and divisions within contemporary culture.

In the next chapter, we have examples of two particular routines delivered by feminist comedians that attracted enormous public controversy. The discussion around both did not, in these cases, originate from the manosphere or other online trolls. Instead, we see a variety of mainstream commentators trying to gain control of the conversational ball and to define and redefine core concepts like femininity, propriety, and motherhood, all attempting to appropriate the language of feminism as their own.

4

Revulsion

Samantha Bee, Michelle Wolf, and Twin Comedic Controversies

WHEN COMEDIAN SAMANTHA Bee called Ivanka Trump a "feckless cunt" (*Full Frontal,* "ICE") during her show, her studio audience audibly gasped before breaking into applause and whoops of delight. Reactions from those in the press echoed the studio audience's initial shock but none of its enjoyment (unless, of course, one counts the evident satisfaction gained in sternly denouncing another's transgressions). A chorus of voices chimed in to explain that Bee had gone too far. Importantly, remarkably similar condemnations had rung out just a month earlier when comedian Michelle Wolf delivered a scathing and profane takedown of the Trump administration at the White House Correspondents' Association (WHCA) dinner. Both incidents drew intense national scrutiny, attracting attention far beyond the bounds of the comedians' regular audiences, as a broad swath of society attempted to make sense of the controversies, simultaneously working through cultural ideals and boundaries.

While growing diversity in comedy (of comics and topics) has generated backlash from generalized audiences, audiences for regular television programs tend to be fairly self-selecting, particularly as the industry has moved further into narrowcasting—aiming programs at small, specific audiences rather than at the general public. This means that with the exception of a small number of ardent misogynists who might watch a program in order to troll it, most average viewers who would potentially be turned off by a particular performer are unlikely to hear much of that comedian's material on a regular basis. However, from time to time, comedic controversies explode into public consciousness, drawing media attention and attracting the focus of many who might not otherwise follow the performer in question. Giselinde Kuipers refers to such blowups as "humor scandals," explaining that these "public controversies about transgressive humor—are recurring events in media democracies, playing out social divides through a dramatization of moral and political rifts" (Kuipers 64). During these humor scandals, commentators of all stripes seem compelled to stake a position, often seizing on the comedian's original statements and using them to speak for their own particular worldview or interests. In the discussion of the comedy, there is much more that informs the dispute than simple opinions about a joke. Such discussions are windows into wider cultural struggles, including those over gender, race, power, and public space.

I examine two such moments that happened in quick succession in the spring of 2018: both Samantha Bee's insult of Ivanka Trump on her program *Full Frontal with Samantha Bee* and Michelle Wolf's performance at the WHCA dinner, particularly her jokes about Sarah Huckabee Sanders, the Trump administration's representative at the dinner. In both cases, there were multiple layers of discursive contestation. Sarah Huckabee Sanders and, to a lesser extent, Ivanka Trump were spokespeople for a particular political administration, meaning that they invariably aimed to advance the narrative framework that the Trump administration was disseminating, largely by repeating approved talking points and defending official policies. As political comedians and satirists, Bee and Wolf took their opportunities to critically reframe some of what Sanders and Ivanka Trump had been doing and saying in the public eye, deconstructing the official pronouncements and policy positions, as well as these figures' performance of self. Once their comedy routines attracted notoriety, a wide variety of public figures and media commentators stepped in to assert control over the narrative, speaking for Bee and Wolf by selectively interpreting and repurposing their jokes while often also speaking on behalf of Sanders and Trump. Transposed from the original performed routines on television (and in front of a live audience), the discussion on cable news, the blogosphere, and social media focused on one or two jokes, divorced from the context of performance, allowing commentators to largely ignore the critical content of the comedy and instead focus on the propriety of the vulgar language employed or on the supposed anger and rudeness of the performers. Finally, the comedians themselves spoke back to the controversies, replying on social media and on their own programs.

In her response, Bee explicitly evoked the specter of censorship, comically presenting a panel of older men who had been tasked with dubbing over her more profane utterances when she found herself getting angry.

The original jokes were overlaid with layer on layer of interpretations as each speaker scrambled for narrative control. Undergirding both comedic crises was, of course, the fact that each gave particular political actors and parties the chance to take shots at one another. But in the wider conversation that unfolded, and the myriad voices that weighed in, there was also a much broader struggle over ideals and norms. What transpired in both cases was a battle over conceptions of femininity and motherhood and, ultimately, over how to be a woman in the public sphere. The media controversy that followed focused narrowly on the perceived appropriateness, vulgarity, and rudeness of the comedic material. It was largely framed as a fight between the individual comedians and the victims of their jokes. Commentators indignantly defended or vilified each half of the comic/victim pair. What the public witnessed, then, was a mediated "catfight" between women in the public eye. And while the spotlight was trained on these two pairs of white women, the real issues and the substance of the critique dropped from view, particularly the injustices suffered by the immigrant families being forcibly separated at the border (the topic of Bee's segment) as well as the powerful men setting the policies in motion, demonstrating the ideological rerouting that occurs in public discussion when the focus remains on women's embodied behavior. Nevertheless, these twin controversies do provide examples of the way in which feminist comics are attempting to change these dynamics by pushing back against conceptions of what it means to be a female performer. In that struggle, between the comedians and their supporters on the one hand and the forces of popular misogyny on the other, we can see a miniature version of the culture wars playing out at lightning speed, a push and pull between those testing the limits of public expectations for female performers and the powerful backlash that such performances can engender.

Industry Changes

The realm of late-night comedy has historically been one of the most stubbornly homogeneous corners of the already conservative television industry. During the network era in particular, the common wisdom was that men had possession of the family's remote control after the children went to bed, meaning that the programming should be aimed at them. While female hosts reigned in daytime talk shows, late-night hosts were white and male. As discussed, even though Joan Rivers was a popular guest host for Johnny Carson, Carson himself would not consider her as a permanent replacement when he retired. Cable television ushered in a smidgeon of diversity when Arsenio Hall, a Black comic, was given his own program in 1989. However, the uniformity of the vast majority of hosts was still so overwhelming that Stephen Colbert was notably the first Catholic (white, male) host when he began *The Colbert Report* in 2005. The number of late-night-style shows has mushroomed of late, spanning both traditional television networks and streaming services. With that growth has come some greater diversity, though the majority of the new shows have not achieved the sort of prominence that previous late-night programs enjoyed. Meanwhile, many of the larger platforms have been slow to change.

In early 2015, when Jon Stewart announced his upcoming retirement from *The Daily Show*, Samantha Bee, as one of the show's popular longtime correspondents, was listed by numerous industry commentators as an obvious choice as successor. The hosting job eventually went to Trevor Noah, a South African comedian who was relatively unknown in the United States. Years later, Bee revealed that Comedy Central had not considered her for the position at all (Sharf). A few months after Bee left *The Daily Show* upon Stewart's impending retirement, TBS offered Bee her own program, which became *Full Frontal with Samantha Bee* (2016–22). As Bee's show was getting ready to launch, in November 2015, *Vanity Fair* magazine tweeted out a picture from its upcoming article celebrating the "titans" of late-night television. The picture they included was of ten men (eight of whom were white) in dark suits, most holding what appear to be tumblers of whiskey. People reacting to the tweet overwhelmingly pointed to the glaring lack of women in the photo. About an hour later, Samantha Bee tweeted the same photo, only she had superimposed a picture of herself as a centaur with lasers for eyes into the middle of the group. The accompanying tweet read "BETTER." Her picture became something of a sensation, with thousands retweeting it, likely because it spoke so satisfyingly to the stark sexism of the original photo. Indeed, her program seemed like it would be fundamentally changing something in the late-night comedy world. The same year that *Full Frontal* premiered (in early 2016), Chelsea Handler also launched a late-night-style talk show on Netflix, while Robin Thede debuted a program of her own a year later on BET, followed by Michelle Wolf creating a Netflix show and also being tapped to host the

WHCA dinner in 2018. Indeed, though none of these programs were on the flagship networks, the hosting gigs were materializing. However, when two of these women used profanity and innuendo to mercilessly attack figures in the Trump administration, they soon found themselves caught in the glare of public scrutiny in a very different manner than any of their male colleagues had experienced.

Comedic Controversies

At the time Michelle Wolf had been hired to provide the entertainment for the WHCA dinner, her star had been rising as a performer, but she was still not widely known. She had been a contributor on several late-night comedy programs and had a successful stand-up special. Her new program on Netflix was set to debut several weeks after the dinner. Unlike Samantha Bee, who was used to speaking to a niche liberal audience on her program and who seemed somewhat blindsided by her routine being catapulted to the center of the national conversation, Wolf, like performers at past WHCA dinners, had a more unpredictable potential audience and had to calibrate her performance accordingly. On the one hand, the live audience at these events is as insular as can be, populated by politicians and political journalists, far removed from the lives of most citizens. On the other hand, if a routine is seen as noteworthy by those journalists in attendance, it can receive heavy coverage and generate significant buzz for the performer. In addition, the event provides a rare opportunity for political comics to address their jokes directly to their targets. As Jonathan P. Rossing points out of past WHCA dinners, "the comic tone of the roast and the atmosphere of the dinner give the guest stand-up roastmasters license to speak directly to power" ("Live from D.C." 170). The choice to fully exercise that license, however, is what some viewers objected to so vehemently in Wolf's routine.

Wolf made the choice to come out swinging that night, going after individual policymakers and media players alike. From the start, she signaled that she would not be sparing anyone's sensibilities, announcing, "Like a porn star says when she's about to have sex with a Trump, 'Let's get this over with'" ("2018 White House Correspondents' Association Dinner"). She made no attempt to put the audience of politicians and reporters at ease, and indeed, some of her jokes were met with uneasy titters and seat shifting by those in the room. This was not an unintentional misfire. Rather, her critique was clearly for the benefit of the home viewers, not her immediate audience. Noting that Trump was not at the event, she quipped, "I would drag him here myself, but it turns out the President of the United States is the one pussy you're not allowed to grab." She followed this quip with, "He said it first. Yeah, he did."

Like Stephen Colbert's infamous roast of George W. Bush's policies at the same event in 2006, during which he also made his immediate audience visibly uncomfortable, Wolf lobbed comedic grenades at the conduct of the administration's representative attending the dinner—in Colbert's case that was Bush himself; in Wolf's, it was Sarah Huckabee Sanders—both of whom had to absorb the criticism while also on camera. Indeed, this was one of the two facets of Wolf's performance that critics reacted to with shock and outrage, the other being her use of profanity and sexual innuendo. Not incidentally, Colbert's roast of Bush also became a heated topic of debate, though for entirely different reasons than Wolf's did. While Wolf was roundly castigated for meanly insulting Sanders in person, in Colbert's case, the controversy was over the fact that he had audaciously spoken his scorching critique in front of Bush and none of the news outlets had initially reported on it. A few fans who had watched the performance on CSPAN began circulating the speech, which was picked up by those on the political left who were greatly relieved and pleased that some of the things they were feeling were finally being articulated in the public sphere, and to Bush's face no less. It became a viral phenomenon and spawned a website called "Thank You Stephen Colbert" that logged tens of thousands of thank-yous in just a few days. Meanwhile, fans accused the media of attempting to cover up the speech by not widely reporting it, eventually sparking a discussion of the perceived inadequate coverage in the press (Day 80–81).

Many in the media explained themselves by saying that they just had not thought the speech was funny, as no one in the room had been laughing. Once the footage had circulated more widely, some supporters of President Bush eventually spoke up to say that they thought Colbert's performance had been rude, but no one suggested that he be sanctioned. In contrast, Wolf's routine was met with immediate shock and finger-wagging outrage by many on both the political right and left, initially sparked by figures in the media. The fallout included the WHCA deciding to cancel the comedy portion of the evening at subsequent dinners (though that prohibition only lasted for three years, two of which involved no dinner at all due to the COVID-19 pandemic).

Much of the indignation was on Sanders's behalf. Wolf referred to her as Aunt Lydia from the television program *The Handmaid's Tale* (adapted from

Figure 4.1. Michelle Wolf at the 2018 White House Correspondents' Association dinner, telling a joke about Sarah Huckabee Sanders.

Margaret Atwood's novel), a character known for enforcing a regime of brutal misogyny and cruelty. Wolf told a joke about Sanders's affect resembling that of a bullying softball coach when Sanders spoke to members of the press, and another about her being the Uncle Tom of disappointing white women. The line that attracted the most outrage was "I actually really like Sarah. I think she's very resourceful. She burns facts, and then she uses that ash to create a perfect smoky eye. Like maybe she's born with it, maybe it's lies. It's probably lies." Many who were offended implied that the jokes had been about Sanders's appearance, an implication that seems to be either a willful misreading or a misunderstanding, as the barb in each of the bits was aimed at the work that Sanders is doing for the Trump administration, which Wolf implied involves lying, bullying, and actively working against the interests of other women. In fact, the only complimentary part of Wolf's routine was the bit explicitly about Sanders's appearance: namely, that Sanders had nicely crafted eye makeup (polished on the outside but rotten on the inside).

Nevertheless, the tone of the criticism was set by the (nominally liberal) commentator Mika Brzezinski who tweeted early the next morning that "watching a wife and mother be humiliated on national television for her looks is deplorable. . . . WHCA owes Sarah an apology." That particular tweet was

Figure 4.2. Sarah Huckabee Sanders reacting to Michelle Wolf's jokes about her.

repeated in many subsequent articles, and its logic was taken up in the cable news conversations. A number of mainstream journalists painted a picture of Sanders as grace under fire, a model of courage and gentility in the face of an attack on her dignity. The trope about Sanders being a wife and mother was also repeated especially enthusiastically by right-wing commentators. That was not an accident. Many of these defenses of Sanders functioned as a subtle reassertion of traditional femininity in the face of Wolf's seemingly aggressive and profane attack.

This line of thinking can be dressed as a form of feminism; indeed, Brzezinski, for one, went on to tweet, "I have experienced insults about my appearance from the President. All women have a duty to unite when these attacks happen" (glossing over the fact that she was defending that same president's representative). But this solidarity discourse also reasserts conservative norms around gender roles, invoking the woman as Madonna, who needs to be shielded from the roughness of the public sphere, and, in the process, reasserting historical ideals of female purity and fragility. Indeed, as Rebecca J. Cook and Simone Cusack explain of global gender ideals, "the stereotypes that women should be mothers, and homemakers, and therefore be 'the center of home and family life' have had a long history of use to justify women's exclusion from public life, such as their ability to hold or stand for public office and to serve on juries" (22). Being yoked to one's maternality has rarely functioned to expand women's rights and freedoms; rather, it has routinely been depicted as a "natural" function that needs to be protected, whether that is helpful to the women in question or not.

Wolf's routine was seized on by commentators on both the left and right who suddenly divorced Sanders from her conduct as a spokesperson for the administration and positioned the routine as an unfair attack on a poised, delicate woman just minding her own business. Since so many had leaped to Sanders's defense, Sanders herself did not have to say much about the routine—indeed, she could not if she were to maintain the unsullied high ground, but she did say of Wolf: "I hope that she can find some of the same happiness that we all have, because I think she may need a little bit more of that in her life because the rest of us here are doing great" (Hains). Although it could have been inadvertent, Sanders's comment conjures the image of Wolf as the bitter feminist, sour at the world because of her own unhappiness (presumably caused by her lack of desirability to men). This image stands in stark contrast to that of the innocent wife and mother under attack that Sanders's defenders invoked. Indeed, it falls into the long history of creating dichotomies for acceptable female behavior. Most of these dichotomies pit the idealized mother against her denigrated opposite: for instance, mothers and spinsters or mothers and whores. The spinster (the figure invoked by Sanders to diminish Wolf) is both pathetic and potentially suspect, while the whore is attractive but dangerous. As Sydney White explains, originating in medieval church dogma, the mother/whore dichotomy refers "to the idea of woman as a mother and woman as a sexual and sexualised being. The former is viewed as the virtuous of the pair, whereas the whore is a double-edged sword: simultaneously attractive and 'evil'" (2). The negative side of this particular dichotomy comes into sharper focus when we turn to the reactions engendered by the off-color language used by both comics. Whether or not Sanders would normally be thought of as delicate or "pure" is largely irrelevant, as the mother moniker (particularly a mother under attack) automatically bestows on her the position of moral superiority.

Not incidentally, the same topics—motherhood, femininity, and morality—were also the initial focus of the Samantha Bee routine that attracted so much attention. The segment had been about the newly developing practice of separating migrant children from their parents at the border, when Bee segued to the fact that Ivanka Trump had just posted an idyllic photo of herself

Figure 4.3. On her program *Full Frontal with Samantha Bee*, Bee does a segment on Ivanka Trump and the immigration policies of her father, President Trump.

with her young son on Instagram. First calling the post "oblivious," Bee then addressed the younger Trump directly, saying, "You know, Ivanka, that is a beautiful photo of you and your child, but let me just say, one mother to another, do something about your dad's immigration practices, you feckless cunt! He listens to you" (*Full Frontal*, "ICE").

Setting her language aside for a moment, at the heart of Bee's critique is her long-standing narrative about Ivanka Trump, who is permitted to embody the most unthreatening version of empowered womanhood. Beautiful and entitled, she has power without being seen as unpleasant. She also has the resources to be both a working woman and a mother without making many sacrifices. And as Amanda Hess put it in the *New York Times*, "Ivanka has always tried to use her status as a woman and a mother to soft-pedal her father's aims, to pink-wash them in vaguely feminist sentiments and feminine images without actually accomplishing any pro-family policy" (Bennett). The bit points to the hypocrisy of Ivanka's public performance of motherhood. Bee is implying that Ivanka may be a mother, but she is a monstrous one if she can nuzzle with her child for the camera while simultaneously not batting an eyelash about other children being ripped from their mothers' arms. In Bee's telling, a mother is not someone with impeccable morality simply by virtue of her practiced domesticity and tenderness. A mother with power must also perform her morality; her failure to do so means that the public display of her motherhood is nothing but a smokescreen meant to obscure the public's view of her father's family-destroying policies.

However, while that critique is relatively legible within the confines of her program, it was entirely eclipsed in the discussion on social media and in the news coverage, the majority of which did not include footage of the original segment. As Sangeet Kumar explains, "media events in a networked world are on a feedback-loop of relentless course correction in response to what is being reported" (544). If the initial commentators say that the import of a given story is the vulgarity employed, that, of course, becomes the story that everyone must weigh in on. Thus, in the case of Bee's segment, the critique of Ivanka and the family separation practices was immediately drowned out by indignation over Bee's use of the word *cunt*. Indeed, it is an incendiary word, with misogynistic roots. Bee later acknowledged this history in her apology, explaining that she had been trying to reclaim the word but now recognized that wielding it as an insult against another woman was not an effective way to do so. Ultimately, using the word provides an easy target, giving one's opponents the opportunity to paint one as a bully. Beyond being described as mean, though, Bee was also treated with shocked disgust. This is again where the two controversies overlap. Both women were referred to by members of the administration (including by the president himself) as "filthy" (Flynn). That, of course, is consistent with Trump's description of other women he deems too aggressive, disloyal, or impolite as "nasty," but he was far from the only one using such terms. Other popular words used by the press to describe either Wolf or Bee included *vile* and *disgusting* (Shanley). The implication in much of the commentary on both performances was that the unrestrained use of swear words and sexual innuendo entirely invalidated whatever critique either comic was making while marking the performers themselves as outside the boundaries of polite society. Never mind, of course, that similar language is routinely used in much mainstream comedy, including on many of the other late-night programs currently on television, or that President Trump himself had been heard using crude slang words for female genitalia while boasting of enacting sexual violence.

On behalf of the administration, Sarah Huckabee Sanders responded to Bee's insult of Ivanka Trump by saying that the "disgusting comments and show are not fit for broadcast and executives at Time Warner and TBS must demonstrate that such explicit profanity about female members of this Administration will not be condoned on its network" (Jenkins). The flagging of Bee's remark being an attack on a *female* member of the administration was deliberate. In both cases, Bee and Wolf were effectively accused of being antifeminist hypocrites for attacking other women. And once again, there was an implicit assertion that the nice kind of women deserve special protection in public debate. Wolf obliquely addressed the antifeminist accusation a few weeks later on the first episode of her program. She did an unrelated segment called "Top 5 Women I Am Not Supporting Right Now," at the end of which she quipped, "I'm not supporting any of them. That doesn't make me any less of a feminist; it just makes me a bitch" (*The Break*, "Strong Female Lead").

Notably, there were voices defending both Wolf and Bee from the torrents of criticism each received. The loudest of these defenses tended to come from other comedians, many of whom pointed out that these women were each just doing their jobs—and, indeed, using provocative language or insulting members of the administration is a routine part of that job. For instance, Dave Chapelle related that he thought Michelle Wolf had "nailed it" (Jacobson), and Jon Stewart attempted to dismiss the controversy over Bee's remark as a "ploy by the right to stir up contrived outrage" (Bradley). But the news cycle narrative that raced ahead in both cases was of a female performer who had clearly taken things too far, and that was the narrative that stuck in most of the mainstream reportage.

Both Bee and Wolf fit the description of what Kathleen Karlyn Rowe has famously termed "unruly women," women who flaunt the social restrictions around female behavior and appearance, which require a controlled and aestheticized body, one that is not too loose, too fat, too relaxed, too crude, or too loud. As Rowe explains, "women are expected to keep not only their bodies but their utterances unobtrusive" (63), restraining and disciplining their public selves. Vulgarity, outspokenness, and sloppiness are considered particularly unseemly in women. There seems to be a direct line between these expectations and the explicit prohibitions around female participation in the bourgeois public sphere discussed in the introduction. As Nancy Henley noted several decades ago, "female voices are expected to be soft and quiet," and women who do not conform are often called loud, "a word commonly applied derogatorily to other minority groups or out-groups" (Henley and Freeman). Indeed, one of the most popular adjectives used to diminish female speakers is *shrill*, a word that implies that the woman's voice is both too loud and unpleasantly high-pitched. That particular insult is still ubiquitous in public discourse and was used repeatedly in reportage of Hillary Clinton's candidacy for president in 2016, for example. However, onlookers now more frequently point it out as problematically misogynist, particularly as more unapologetically feminist women gain public platforms with which to communicate their own critique. American writer and humorist Lindy West has attempted to reclaim the term for women who speak up for themselves, naming her 2016 essay collection *Shrill: Notes from a Loud Woman*, which was subsequently adapted into a television show simply titled *Shrill* (2019–21).

Similarly, the charge of being unpleasant to listen to is one that both Samantha Bee and Michelle Wolf preemptively embrace in their comedy, happily laying ownership to the "shrillness" of which they anticipate being accused. Wolf, for instance, makes no attempt to soften the register of her unusual voice, perhaps even playing up its screechiness. On the first episode of her (now canceled) show *The Break*, she began with, "Yes, this is my real voice, so I'd like to welcome you and, I'm assuming, your dogs" (*The Break*, "Strong Female Lead"). For her part, Bee presents it as a given that her very presence will be offensive to some and makes clear that she will make no attempt to soften her edges or temper her style, explaining, "There are plenty of people who won't tune in because a woman's voice bothers their eardrums. Their ear canals can't handle the sound of my shrill voice talking at them about a subject. I guess I just don't really care about those people" (Traister). Indeed, Bee does not just ignore the rules of female behavior but also draws attention to and mocks them while also making it a regular habit of shining a spotlight on the insults and rage both she and many other women in the public eye are subjected to.

Bee has devoted a number of segments on *Full Frontal with Samantha Bee* (2016–22) to the vitriol directed at publicly vocal women. She also developed a running gag on her "web extras" provided for fans online, which was a game whose object is for her to try to discern whether a particular piece of her own hate mail is real or if it has been fabricated by her staff. She thus defangs the insults and threats of violence through humor, rendering her harassers laughable. Bee's other tactic is to turn the troll's language back on the troll in a trick of comedic jujitsu. She co-opts the florid insults of the internet, usurping them as a form of power directed back at those who would use them to diminish and intimidate. While (almost) never importing the sexism, racism, or other forms of bigotry so common on the internet, she luxuriates in the baroquely embellished put-down. Both Bee and Wolf, in fact, are talented insult comics. Near the start of her program, Bee, for instance, referred to first candidate and then president Trump (a favorite target), as, among other things, "a sentient caps-lock button" (February 9, 2016), "a crotch-fondling slab of rancid meatloaf" (October 5, 2016), and a "leaky whoopee cushion full of expired cottage cheese who threatens to erode the very foundations of our liberal democracy" (December 20, 2016). Similarly, in the midst of her frustration over the Trump administration's family separations at the border, Wolf staged her own "teeny roast" of the responsible policymakers in which she implied that then attorney general Jeff Sessions's grandfather was "a burning cross" and said of White House adviser Stephen Miller, "You look like if Joseph Goebbels stopped taking Propecia" (*The Break*, "Entertainment Explosion").

Rather than attempt to appeal to a wide audience by tempering their style in light of expectations of women, both comics are unapologetically fierce, frequently drawing attention to those expectations and gleefully giving them the middle finger. When addressing their own audiences (presumably a self-selecting crowd), both performers seem to assume that their viewers will enjoy their targeting of legislation, traditions, and individuals that work against equality of all types, especially gender inequality. In fact, because an unabashedly outspoken feminist voice is still such a rarity on television, part of the appeal of such comedy is that it provides a shared space of affirmation and strength. Because both performers frequently align themselves with a feminist viewpoint, they easily become objects of identification (or disidentification) for viewers. Even when not speaking about gender in particular, the "unruliness" of their style of performance is clear. While women who transgress are typically subject to social judgment and punishment, the shock they elicit also demonstrates "the disruptive power of the unruly woman" (Rowe 54). Such is absolutely the case in both comedic controversies profiled here. However, we should bear in mind, as Anne Helen Petersen explains, that even grudgingly tolerated unruliness "is still largely the provenance of women who are white and straight," which likely explains why, of all comics, it is Bee and Wolf who have felt that they could push against gendered boundaries so forcefully (xx).

In their reactions to both controversies, most commentators, whether they were conscious of it or not, were weighing in not just on a comedy routine but on acceptable forms of femininity in the public sphere. All of the descriptions of the jokes as vile and disgusting call to mind Mary Douglas's classic anthropological work on dirt. Surveying cross-cultural understandings of the concept, Douglas famously defines dirt simply as "matter out of place." In these particular examples, we have women out of place. Both Bee and Wolf are feminist women aggressively using comic profanity and innuendo in the public sphere while turning their unruly aggression on good wives and mothers. Snippets of each comedy routine were repeated in bowdlerized form, changing their meaning. Divorced from their critical content in this way, they were positioned as uncontrollable outbursts of filthy innuendo.

Ventriloquized by the offended commentators, the profanity became evidence of the comedians' unwarranted aggressiveness and unnatural depravity, qualities that should presumably be at odds with their femaleness. The fact that the vulgarity seemed mixed with passionate conviction made it all the more off-putting for some onlookers. As Rebecca Krefting explains, "When women use humor as social critique, it gets labeled as 'angry' and 'humorless,' which means that men's humor counts as humor while women's humor counts as anger" ("Hannah Gadsby: On the Limits of Satire" 100). A writer for the right-wing publication *Daily Caller* put all of this explicitly, using Michelle Wolf's performance to excoriate "self-hating feminists" and arguing that "lefty feminists seem to measure their 'power' and 'agency' by their success in aping the worst of male behavior, even as they treat men (and the unborn) with contempt" and that "they define themselves by what they reject, and alienate themselves from traditional aspects of womanhood: motherhood, femininity, sensitivity, and self-giving love" (Hasson). The writer's argument is essentially that feminism itself is unnatural and perverse, an ideology that entails a rejection of a woman's natural motherly virtues. While this commentator is more explicit and extreme, even the mainstream ones were, to some degree, policing both what can be said *about* women and *by* women.

Everyone was hoping to control the more obvious political narrative as to whose team had been publicly embarrassed, but part of that narrative was also about how to be a woman in public. While there was a minority of commentators, along with other performers, publicly defending both Bee and Wolf in the name of comedy and critique, those voices could hardly counter the dominant media framing device of out-of-control female comic rudely and excessively attacking public figures. Implicitly depicted as polar opposites, the choice was between a femaleness that is graceful, selfless, and contained or one that is loud, crude, wanton, and angry—a lady or a shrew, a mother or a whore.

Femininity, Motherhood, and Race

Of course, a discussion about women and motherhood is premised on the assumption that there are children involved. In these controversies, the children (of either the performers or the members of the administration) remained largely abstracted or absent from the conversation. Public debates about femininity and motherhood tend to center on mothers as theoretical reproductive vessels, rather than on the needs of individual children. Mothers are tasked with raising the next generation, and implicitly with reproducing the current order, including the power dynamics and hierarchies already firmly in place. Social messages about motherhood are inevitably inflected by the race and class of the imagined or real mother. Katherine Kinnick points out that "media narratives often cast motherhood in moral terms, juxtaposing the 'good mother' with the 'bad mother,' who frequently is a working mom, a lower income mom, or someone who does not conform to traditional gender roles of behavior, ambition, or sexual orientation" (4). Mothers of color are frequently demonized for producing too many children or for doing a poor job of raising their children. This form of vilification stands in stark contrast to the idealized constructions of white, middle-class motherhood, which is associated with the reproduction of the "right" kind of children. Sanders and Ivanka Trump are the right kind of mother, and they were seen as under attack. While you could arguably posit that the innuendo about Wolf being unhappy was a coded reference to her status as a childless woman, Samantha Bee's performance as a mother (she has three children) did not become a focus of the media conversation, perhaps because she had already been placed in the category of depraved aggressor in opposition to saintly motherhood.

What is striking about both comedic controversies, though, is the way in which the idealized white mothers are held up as paragons of virtue because of their status as mothers, while the brown mothers (and fathers) who had been separated from their children and were being held in cages and mass detention centers were entirely overlooked. The concern expressed about mothers was clearly only about a particular kind of mother, one who is ultimately responsible for the reproduction of whiteness. Preoccupations with reproducing the right kind of children have long remained unconscious or at least unspoken directly. However, the currently ascendant alt-right—which is often

intertwined with popular misogyny and the manosphere—has been working hard to fan anxieties that white people, and white men in particular, are
somehow under siege or threatened by multiculturalism. As Viveca Greene
details, the proliferation of memes and Twitter conversations created under
the hashtag #whitegenocide deliberately "amplifies and inflates the discourse
of reverse racism and engenders fear among whites that immigration, interra-
cial relationships and children, and diversity initiatives and practices (among
other public and private forms of racial integration) are leading to the elimina-
tion of whites" ("'Deplorable' Satire" 51), a fear that the Trump administration happily stoked as justification for the immigration policies in question.
As these discourses become more mainstream, their influence extends into
popular cultural debates around seemingly unrelated topics, including, for
instance, what is appropriate material for a comedy routine. Here immigrant
mothers are not visible as mothers, because they have been thoroughly coded
as invaders and criminals.

While the way the two comedic controversies were discussed was similar,
the one major difference between them was that when Wolf's jokes were repeated in subsequent articles, they necessarily retained some of their critical
content, while the material about Bee tended to simply allude to the crude
term she had used without retaining her critique about Ivanka Trump or
about the cruelty of the administration's immigration policy. In Bee's apology
on her program the following week, she related that she felt remorse particularly because the term she had used had distracted from discussion of the
immigration policy. After apologizing for her choice of words, she then went
on to self-consciously dramatize the experience of having her comedy policed
by media commentators, taking the opportunity to make a point both about
the controversy and about women's voices.

In the ensuing follow-up segment on the child-separation story, Bee opens
by introducing her audience to some "exciting new additions" to her show: a
panel of older men in suits who will be serving as the show's new "mandatory
censors" (Full Frontal, "Missing Migrant"). Each time Bee gets upset (again
about the stories of inhumane cruelty unfolding at the border), the men push
the buttons in front of them, which dub over Bee's voice with comically non-
sensical phrases that sound similar to the swear words she might have used.
While making it clear that the government's policies are still monstrous and
upsetting (the important story), she also draws attention to the uproar over
the civility of her language, literalizing the attempt to referee and reshape her

utterances in the form of a group of humorless men who would reign in her unruly outbursts. Within the comedic space of the program, she can flip the stereotypical script, painting the male would-be censors as the killjoys who seek to police, while the feminist speaker fights valiantly to speak truth to power. It was a segment that was undoubtedly not seen by as many people as had heard about her insult of Ivanka, but was one that provided further critique and catharsis for her fans.

Both Wolf and Bee sought to remind their audiences of the real-world effects set in motion by the powerful figures they were mocking. After Wolf had finished her monologue at the WHCA dinner and had said "good night," she leaned back into the microphone and shouted "Flint still doesn't have clean water!" Both comics ultimately attempted to remind the audience that, more than anything, they were striving to point out terrible injustices in the country, injustices that should be the ultimate focus of conversation and source of offense.

Conclusion

In both comedic controversies, feminist comedians created routines designed to express their anger over great wrongs. In both cases, however, public discussions over the immorality of the policies in question were largely drowned out by pronouncements on the immorality of the language and the civility of the performers. Such visceral reactions to a joke and to the joke teller reveal not simply political leanings but fundamental instincts about gender roles and the "appropriateness" of behavior for particular bodies.

The two controversies make visible the battles between popular feminism and popular misogyny that Banet-Weiser documents, though in these cases, many more onlookers were drawn in than are normally prime players in this war. Banet-Weiser notes that these struggles often become focused on women's bodies, usually those of heteronormative, cisgendered white women, the value of which are "constantly deliberated over, surveilled, evaluated, judged, and scrutinized through media discourses, law, and policy" (28), as seen everywhere from misogynistic online comments to love-your-body discourses and corporate empowerment campaigns. In these cases, we see how the obsession with women's performed behavior can overshadow all other concerns, including the issues raised by these particular comedians.

Nevertheless, despite the very real wave of indignation that crashed down on the performers, both remain unbowed in their convictions, and both continue to have quite successful comedy careers (though both have subsequently lost their television programs, which we will return to in the conclusion). There are clearly many who are eager to hear these comics' critiques and, as evidenced by Bee's studio audience, will happily applaud their trash-talking. Indeed, in addition to revealing the powerful forces that would attempt to censor feminist voices, the incidents also demonstrate the way in which feminist comedy is challenging taboos and norms while it provides an object of identification for many fans. These performers seem to have touched a nerve, ultimately highlighting the ongoing cultural friction around conceptions of respectable femininity and motherhood. The controversies also very clearly drive home the fact that female performers have become hot spots in the culture wars, themselves sites of battle over ideals of gender and power, providing us with a revealing glimpse into where the fault lines lie and what battles have yet to be won.

5

Hope

Hannah Gadsby and the Expansion of Comedy's Borders

WHEN STAND-UP COMEDIAN Hannah Gadsby[1] first created their comedy special *Nanette*, in which they reveal past traumas, display their anger, and craft long stretches of the show to be joke free, they assumed that it would end their career. They break many of the comedy rules and point-edly do not comply with the expectations for female performers, drawing attention to how damaging those rules and expectations are. They use the form of stand-up comedy to critique the industry of stand-up comedy. Thus, they announce early in the set that they are quitting comedy, as they dispassionately watch their bridges burn behind them. To their surprise, however, the special instead launched them to stardom. In addition to winning awards and accolades, the show became one of the most talked-about comedy specials of all time, sparking innumerable articles and a great deal of cultural reflection. While they received some mild backlash in the moment, there was also a fierce outpouring of support for them and for the messages they aimed to convey. In this final case study, rather than the nasty cultural battles we have witnessed around our other performers, we see instead a sudden tidal wave of interest in changing the notoriously male-dominated industry of stand-up comedy. Here Gadsby becomes a

---

1. When performer Hannah Gadsby first rose to fame with *Nanette*, they used she/her pro-nouns. Since then, they have shifted to using they/them pronouns. I use they/them pronouns throughout this volume in deference to Gadsby's preferences, though some of the quotations I have included from other commentators use "she/her" as they were written several years before this book was published.

popular cultural touchstone for many of the feelings that had previously remained inchoate or unarticulated within the mainstream.

Originally from Tasmania, Gadsby began their career as a performer after entering and winning a comedy competition in 2006 and subsequently appearing in the Edinburgh Fringe Festival. In the intervening years before debuting *Nanette*, Gadsby wrote for and appeared in several Australian television programs and continued performing stand-up comedy, developing a reputation primarily in the Australian region. But it was *Nanette*, first existing as a touring show (in 2017–18) and then a Netflix comedy special (2018), that brought Gadsby international fame and made them the center of a number of soul-searching cultural conversations in much of the English-speaking world. *Nanette* was followed by another live-show-turned-Netflix-special in 2019 and 2020 called *Douglas*, which received a good deal of press coverage and was again well reviewed, though it did not spark quite the same number of think pieces, debates, and general buzz (a feat that would have been extremely difficult to replicate, particularly since no one had anticipated the impact that *Nanette* ended up having). They have continued to tour and produce specials since then.

I am particularly interested in the discourse around *Nanette*. Because the special was hugely talked about, important questions then include why so many people were interested and what the larger discussion can tell us. That conversation is of course firmly rooted in the particular moment at which *Nanette* was released, so what can viewers' reactions demonstrate about the moment? Notably, much of the discourse, both praising and critiquing the special, was mediated through questions of genre—whether *Nanette* counted as comedy, whether it challenged the conventions of comedy or satire, and whether comedy and trauma can coexist. Because genre is where creators and audiences meet with a set of preconceived expectations and options for adaptation, it became a site of struggle for transforming a larger "rape culture" and a sort of proxy cultural battlefield for the larger #MeToo fight. In trying to shape how people reacted to *Nanette*, both Gadsby and their audience were trying to affect how people react to gender more broadly. Arriving at just the right moment, *Nanette* became a popular cultural node of identification (or disidentification) for ongoing conceptual shifts happening simultaneously, demonstrating our need for cultural touchstones to help process, reflect back, and amplify our cultural struggles. By concentrating emotions into an object that people could hold in common, *Nanette* became a means by which to transform the culture itself.

Industry Changes

Stand-up comedy has long been an overwhelmingly white and male industry. Before performers can achieve any notoriety, they must spend countless
hours honing their material in small performance venues. These have historically been fairly inhospitable environments for women. Stand-up comedy
exploded in popularity in the 1980s as clubs specifically devoted to stand-up
popped up all over the country, creating many performance opportunities,
though female performers "faced a distinct set of challenges their male coun-
terparts were spared: sexist club owners, hecklers, and cultural dictates on
what was and wasn't acceptable, ladylike behavior. In many clubs, female
stand-ups were restricted to 'women's nights' or special rooms at the club
that were separate but decidedly not equal" (Kohen 168). At about the same
time, newly developing cable television launched stand-up comedy specials
as a way to generate inexpensive programming. For several decades to follow,
HBO largely controlled which performers were given stand-up specials. Some
women, like Roseanne Barr, were granted a platform, but the vast majority
of specials went to established male comedians. Comedian Elayne Boosler
famously had to finance her own special, *Party of One*, in 1985. Only after it
demonstrated success did Showtime agree to finance more (Love).

However, the advent of streaming platforms has drastically altered the
stand-up comedy landscape by vastly increasing the sheer number of comedy
specials that are made and changing the calculus behind whose work will
be financed. The streaming juggernaut that is Netflix has built its business
model around being the all-channels platform. They provide television and
film content in just about every genre and taste culture, using their algorithm
to keep serving up the products they anticipate individual viewers will desire. As we have seen with other forms of television, this means that it is not
much of a gamble to develop material that is aimed somewhere other than the
mainstream of middle America. Hence, when Hannah Gadsby, a relatively
unknown butch lesbian performer out of Australia, began attracting attention
at the Edinburgh Fringe Festival, Netflix could offer them a special without
significant risk. And Netflix will stand by their performers as long as they
continue to be profitable. So, Hannah Gadsby can be one of their many successful comedy stars, while the company will also happily continue to back
Dave Chapelle, who has drawn significant heat for comedy seen as offensive
to the trans and LGBTQ communities but who is also massively famous and
thus lucrative. In other words, they can offer both the Dave Chappelle channel

and the Hannah Gadsby channel. Be that as it may, however, few would have predicted prior to its release the amount of discussion that would eventually be generated by *Nanette*.

In what follows, I analyze the content of *Nanette*, followed by the discussion that has surrounded it. I also briefly discuss Gadsby's subsequent special *Douglas* and its reception because I think the expectations and desires surrounding what Gadsby would do next are revealing of the dilemmas facing performers who have been elevated to the status of public intellectual.

Nanette

Though there were some differences between the touring version of *Nanette* and the one produced by Netflix, this chapter will focus primarily on the Netflix version, as it is the performance that the majority of audience members saw and the one to which the majority of reviewers, bloggers, fans, and foes were reacting. The framing device for the special is a series of shots of Gadsby arriving at their home, greeting their dogs, and making a cup of tea. It is a surprisingly intimate introduction for a comedy special, one that hints at the personal nature of the material to come. Intercut with the tea making are shots of the cheering crowd at the Sydney Opera House. As the Gadsby in their home lifts their cup and saucer from the counter, the Gadsby on stage finds their place at the microphone. Overlapping these two events sets the stage from the beginning that Gadsby will be blurring the distinction between the private and the public, the home and the stage, recalling the radical feminist dictum that the "personal is political." Perhaps just as importantly, it establishes early on the importance of the audience, suggesting that just as Gadsby takes their "home life" onto the stage, they will also take the stage back home, and so how the crowd reacts is an important part of processing previously private experience. To help shape audience reaction, Gadsby jokes early in the show about how a previous audience member responded to their comedy, giving them a "bit of feedback"—namely, that their routine did not have enough lesbian content. In so doing, they provide a pedagogy for their audience: suggesting ways *not* to respond, as these are shown to be unhelpful and somewhat absurd.

Gadsby begins their routine with a discussion about small towns, segueing into stories about their upbringing. They explain that they feel generally uncomfortable in small towns as a butch lesbian, since they present as "gender not normal." They trace the arc of their coming of age: growing up in Tasmania, Australia, a place where homosexuality was illegal until 1997, and feeling that they had to leave once they realized that they were gay. While circling back several times to the "bit of feedback" about the dearth of lesbian content, they tell an amusing anecdote they had developed for one of their first comedy sets about their mother's insensitive reaction when they came out to her and another about being mistaken for a "faggot" by a pugnacious young man with whose girlfriend Gadsby had been flirting.

Again returning to the complaint that they were not doing enough lesbian content, Gadsby introduces the idea that they should quit comedy (a refrain to which they will return)—first semifacetiously and lightly. They teasingly ask, "What sort of comedian can't even make the lesbians laugh?" And answers, "Every comedian ever." The line gets a hearty laugh, but Gadsby proceeds to deconstruct the joke, pointing to the harmfulness embedded in its humor. They explain that it is an old joke and a bulletproof one, as "the only people who don't think it's funny . . . are us lezzers. . . . But we've got to laugh . . . because if we don't . . . proves the point. Checkmate." Their tone is still light, but they skillfully make a point that many theorists of comedy and satire have argued about humor directed at the disempowered. While the joker can always hide behind the frivolity of humor, as it is "just a joke," the denigrated group is in a double bind, as laughing along can feel like complicity in one's own denigration while "refusal to accept the comic frame is unpleasant and abrasive: people objecting to humour 'spoil the fun,' show they 'can't take a joke' and thus 'have no sense of humour'" (Kuipers 73) (See also Lewis; Bemiller and Schneider).

Gesturing to many of the tired truisms about women and humor, Gadsby quips that the unlaughing lesbians joke was invented a while back, "well before even women were funny," when the definition of a lesbian was "just any woman not laughing at a man." They then assume the voice of a man chiding an unlaughing woman, yelling, "Fucking learn to take a joke. You need to lighten up. I'll tell you what you need to lighten up. You need a good dicking. Get a cock up you! Drink some jizz!" They perform this bit while miming the actions in question, which makes the impression quite comical but also adds a slightly unsettling air of menace. They then repeat, more seriously this time, the assertion that they think they should quit comedy. Interspersed with the jokes, they go on to quite seriously explain that though they had built a career out of self-deprecating humor, they do not want to do that anymore. In spite of the fact that the audience had just laughed at the humorless lesbian joke, the crowd is, at this point, following them so raptly that it breaks into applause at

Figure 5.1. In *Nanette*, Hannah Gadsby explains why they think they need to quit comedy.

this declaration. They go on to explain that for someone who already exists at the margins, self-deprecation is not humility but humiliation. They elaborate, "I put myself down in order to speak, in order to seek permission . . . to speak. And I simply will not do that anymore. Not to myself or anybody who identifies with me. And if that means that my comedy career is over, then so be it." This declaration is met with cheers from the audience. In part, this is because Gadsby has primed the audience to be sympathetic to their experience, taking them into their confidence, sharing their (thus far) comical experiences of homophobia, and interpellating them as people who are smarter than simplistic homophobes or overly demanding fans. It is also delivered as an important announcement.

Though it comes early in the routine and is not the most dramatic of the announcements Gadsby makes in *Nanette*, their declaration about self-deprecation is one that is frequently quoted. The implication to their statement is that there is an industry-wide expectation in comedy that they deliver their material couched in self-deprecation, an expectation that they are publicly disavowing. Indeed, it is true that for female performers in particular, there has long been a tendency toward self-deprecation, as I touch on briefly in the introduction. Because of deep-seated cultural beliefs that women are constitutionally unfunny and that comedy may be too unseemly for women, female comedians have often been viewed with suspicion, if not downright hostility. As Linda Mizejewski and Victoria Sturtevant explain, because "the edginess of comedy is understood to be something unnatural to women" (2), a woman's unruly comic transgressions are pathologized in a way that men's typically are not, working against women's participation in comedy. One strategy that female comedians have often resorted to is self-deprecation as a way of rendering themselves less threatening to mainstream audiences. Frequently this self-deprecation has taken the form of playing up the performer's inability to meet cultural ideals of female beauty and behavior. Similarly, other marginalized groups, nearly all of whom are underrepresented in the comedy industry, a space overwhelmingly dominated by white, cis, able-bodied men, have often turned toward self-deprecation as a performance strategy. Rául Pérez, for instance, documents the way that in stand-up comedy training "non-whites are often encouraged to engage in racial stereotypes uncritically" (478). These are the industry pressures that Gadsby is highlighting and rejecting.

That said, some have chafed at the implication in *Nanette* that self-deprecation is always unequivocally harmful and disempowering. Self-deprecating humor is its own proud tradition for many marginalized groups. Peter Moskowitz, for instance, asserts that it is a uniquely important part of Jewish humor, developed as a way to process trauma, particularly in the wake of the Holocaust. He argues, "Gadsby's claim that self-deprecation is counterproductive is weighted, whether or not she realizes it, with judgement. There is no 'right' way to experience and process trauma. Coming from someone who didn't grow up Jewish, Gadsby getting praise for bad-mouthing self-deprecation strikes me as an erasure of its Jewish roots. It feels, well, disrespectful—maybe even uncivil." While I don't know that any particular group owns self-deprecation, I would assert that the mode has at times been used as a sneaky form of subversion by a variety of marginalized individuals. It is arguably at least an ambivalent mode, one that lends itself to polysemic reading positions, often strategically. As discussed in the introduction, women's self-deprecatory humor is sometimes arguably demeaning, but it has, on the flip side, allowed female comics to publicly acknowledge and discuss the weight of gendered beauty norms and other social expectations for women, acknowledging and mocking how those expectations can harm one's sense of self. It seems clear that there are varying types of self-deprecatory humor and that not all are experienced as a form of humiliation by the outsider comic, meaning that Gadsby's declaration certainly does not hold for all performers.

What is most important about this moment in *Nanette*, however, is how Gadsby attested to finding their own past routines damaging to their sense of self-worth and that they vowed not to do that kind of comedy anymore, despite whatever industry pressures they experienced, while their earlier lesson in the history of the comic denigration of women and lesbians helped the audience sympathize with their position. As I explore, it was this declaration of purpose that many audience members found particularly affirming, a declaration they wanted to both applaud and amplify. While there are certainly other female and queer comics who have managed to successfully navigate the perils of self-deprecation, Gadsby is the one who telegraphed their intentions unequivocally, announcing them to their audience almost as a manifesto, which is why they garnered so much attention.

From there, Gadsby then pivots into more humorous material, using another piece of audience "feedback" that they have received in order to launch into a discussion of how strangely uptight the mainstream (or "gender normals") are about gender, as they ridicule practices such as the placing of pink headbands on bald babies. They also describe their experience of being routinely mistaken for a man at first glance. They laugh at how embarrassed this makes people when they subsequently realize that they are female. They quip that though they are not transgender, they do not mind being mistaken for a man, as it is like a tiny holiday, since "for a few moments, life gets a hell of a lot easier. I'm top-shelf normal, king of the humans. I'm a straight white man. I'm about . . . I'm about to get good service for no fucking effort!" Thus begins an extended segment in which Gadsby launches a series of jokes at straight white men, repeatedly following them with the refrain "just jokes, just jokes." They feign concern for men's current predicament, explaining that it is a confusing time to be a straight white man, since for the first time they are a "subcategory of human." Addressing their comedy to the men in the audience, they say that while the rest of us are used to this, "you fellas . . . Bit soft in the belly. You hear 'straight white man,' you're like, 'No. No, that's reverse sexism.' No, it's not. You wrote the rules. Read them. Just jokes. Banter. Don't feel intimidated. It's just locker room talk."

Gadsby here slyly returns to the old tropes about humorless women while self-consciously appropriating the rhetoric used to dismiss any hurt caused by a joke. As Olu Jenzen points out, "it is not simply a turning of the tables on at whose expense the joke is. Rather it also involves engendering the formula of the misogynist non-serious rhetoric of 'lad' humour, for feminist purposes, directing it towards men" (3). Indeed, they comically push the conceit to its limits, finally advising straight white men that they should probably try to stop being so sensitive and develop a sense of humor about it, suggesting, "You need to lighten up, learn to laugh. Tell you what might help. How about a good dicking? Get a cock up ya, drink some jizz! You gotta laugh!" They then pause as if to reflect for the first time on the fact that this is strange advice: "It's weird. It doesn't... It's not good, is it? It doesn't feel very nice, does it?" It is an economic way to neatly deconstruct the rhetoric around gender and humor that is so commonplace as to be nearly unremarkable, despite its ideological nature. It is also a pleasurable surprise reversal of power. As Jenzen puts it, "Gadsby skillfully plays with naturalised and ubiquitous assumptions about the gendered nature of humourlessness by turning them on their heads. Thus the female/lesbian failure is enacted, queerly, onto the humourless 'fellas' in the audience" (12). I would add that by repeating the more graphic line about "jizz," they also highlight the violence that underlies the dynamic. Like a number of the themes woven through the routine, the violence and menace are elements Gadsby subtly hints at throughout but does not fully explore until the final section.

First, Gadsby launches into a description of how jokes work, characterizing them as a build-up of tension followed by the tension's diffusion through laughter. They say that they learned to be funny as a survival tactic when they were a child, as their very presence produced tension in a room. They also assert that the tension is making them sick, again broaching the idea of quitting comedy but quickly dismissing it. Explaining that they only have a degree in art history, they paint themself as sadly unqualified to do anything but comedy. Digging into that art world expertise, in the remaining half of the show Gadsby weaves together jokes about art history with further revelations about their own personal life. Both strands end up funneling into a dissection of the problems with comedy as it is currently practiced. They assert that in a comedy show, there is no room for the ending of a story. Because one is expected to finish each anecdote on a punchline, comedians typically give the beginning and middle of the story but not the end. They provide the example of their relationship with their mother, who has evolved significantly in her understanding of homosexuality and her relationship with her daughter. However, Gadsby's earlier routines about their mother's reaction to their coming out had frozen the story at its trauma point. They assert that, in fact, they need to make sure to tell their story properly because you learn from the part of the story that you focus on.

They also ask us to think about the stories told by art. Some of this material involves lighter jokes about the women in classical paintings draped bonelessly on random surfaces with a rogue breast hanging out, though they also deliver a more pointed, extended riff on why they hate Pablo Picasso. As they explain, in addition to making misogynist comments, Picasso had a relationship with a seventeen-year-old girl when he was forty-two, which he justified by announcing that they were both "in their prime." Ribbing comedians for going after the easy jokes, they assert that the thing that should be the target of jokes at the moment is "our obsession with reputation." They list a number of male celebrities who have been credibly accused of sexual misconduct, including Picasso, Donald Trump, Harvey Weinstein, Bill Cosby, and Woody Allen, arguing, "They are not individuals, they are our stories. And the moral of our story is, 'We don't give a shit. We don't give a fuck . . . about women or children. We only care about a man's reputation.'" As they follow this topic, they ditch the jokes and allow themself to display anger and then pause to self-consciously reflect on this anger, observing that it is not supposed to be their place to be angry on stage, as that makes them "a miserable lesbian ruining all the fun" (while male comedians performing anger are seen as "heroes of free speech"). Nevertheless, they do not rein in the anger. Instead, they return to the story they had told at the start of the show about the ignorant young man who mistook them for a "faggot." They explain that to turn that story into comedy, they had originally not told the ending: having realized that they were actually a "lady faggot," and therefore outside of the prohibition against hitting women, the man later returned to find them and brutally beat them. They confess that they neither took themself to the hospital nor reported the attack to the police as they felt ashamed, asserting that is what happens when "you soak one child in shame and give permission to another to hate," explaining that being incorrectly gendered is clearly a punishable offense.

By calling abusive men "our story" and then pivoting to their individual experience of violence, Gadsby announces a desire to transform shared responses around male sexual violence through the specifics of their own story. Their embodied, gendered tale confronts the expectations of genre (the common outlines of "our story"), but for the challenge to be effective, they know they must get others to join the "me" in this #MeToo story, which means urging a wider audience to identify with the newly retold "our story." Thus, instead of inserting a joke to dispel the tension as they have earlier, they address the audience, telling them "this tension, it's yours. I am not helping you anymore. You need to learn what this feels like because this . . . this tension is what not-normals carry inside of them all of the time because it is dangerous to be different!" Then they zero in on straight white men in particular, admonishing them to "Pull your fucking socks up! . . . How humiliating! Fashion advice from a lesbian. That is your last joke." And, indeed, the remaining few minutes of the show are raw and mostly unleavened by humor. They explain that despite accusations to the contrary, they do not hate men, but they are afraid of them, as it was a man who beat them up, a man who sexually abused them as a child, and two men who raped them as a young adult. They assert that they did not reveal these details so as to be seen as a victim; rather, they tell them because their story has value. Indeed, their story is what should be "our story" instead of the story of abusive men. They argue, "Laughter is not our medicine. Stories hold our cure." Finally, they say that they do not have the strength to take care of their own story anymore, asking the audience to help them take care of it, concluding that "connection" is the focus of the story that we need. They exit to cheers and applause.

The Limits of Comedy?

In their discussion of the traps they feel that they have fallen into while performing comedy, Gadsby speaks about the need for the comedic performer to dispel tension by provoking a laugh. As discussed, they argue that comics can tell the beginning and middle of a story but not the ending of a difficult tale, as that would break the rules by not making an audience laugh and hence would not dispel the tension. Much like their statements on self-deprecation, this is rooted in a fundamental truth about the norms of the comedy industry, though it likewise is something of an overgeneralization. Stand-up comedy in particular is notoriously uncomfortable for the performer if a given audience fails to laugh. Success (in the eyes of everyone from bookers, to MCs, to audience members) is routinely measured by the frequency with which an audience laughs, while it is standard for hecklers to verbally intimidate performers who are seen to be flailing. That said, there are nevertheless plenty of niches of experimental stand-up that eschew the setup-punchline-repeat structure, while other comics such as Tig Notaro have attracted positive attention by telling harrowing personal stories on stage. But to Gadsby's point, stand-up comedians are traditionally expected to be consistently funny in a way that does not upset audience members, and that expectation has often functioned to discourage particular types of stories and particular voices from finding a home on the comedy stage.

Because of its transgression of the narrative conventions of comedy, and its explicit connection between genre transgression and gender transgression, *Nanette* sparked much discussion about whether it highlighted the limits of comedy as a form. Some of the journalistic articles posit questions about whether comedy is simply unable to deal with trauma. In the academic sphere, Rebecca Krefting ("On the Limits of Satire") argues that *Nanette* demonstrates both the potential and the limitations of satire as a form. I disagree. I don't think Gadsby's critique was about humor, per se, or about satire, jokes, or any other comedic form or genre. Rather, they excoriated the comedy *industry* as an institution (and by extension, the wider culture that created that industry). Krefting writes, "Stand-up comedy delivers its humor through stories, often experiences and observations based on real life. What information and which emotions are omitted from jokes in the service of satire's form? Satire's reliance on a play frame and laughter makes it difficult to include all parts of a story" ("On the Limits of Satire" 97). However, satire scholars have long pointed out that satire need not involve laughter at all (Gray et al.; Day). While it does generally incorporate some sort of wit, play, or artistry, often taking the form of irony, it need not aim for yucks. One of the most enduring examples of satire, Jonathan Swift's *A Modest Proposal*, for instance, could hardly be described as eliciting belly laughs from its audience. Its cavalier descriptions of eating human babies and making their skin into fine leather goods is rightfully horrifying. The only real "joke" in the piece is the idea that anyone would actually support such a proposal. "Satire" is an inherently nebulous form. We do tend to know it when we see it, but we use the word to describe individual texts across a wide variety of media (from literature to theater, television, film, etc.), many of which vary considerably in form. It could hardly be described as a proscriptive or formulaic artistic construction. The same cannot be said for stand-up comedy, which is a far more delimited form, controlled by relatively few gatekeepers. While Gadsby does not ever mention "satire" in their act, they do speak repeatedly about "comedy." As they explain in a *New York Times* interview, "What I was talking about there is club comedy. Because that's the world that built comedy. Our comics come out of this gladiatorial setup/punch line shock" (Marchese). They go on that in order to ascend the ranks in stand-up comedy, one has to come through the clubs, explaining, "I know how to do that. I know how to tear someone a new [expletive]. I don't feel good about it. I don't like going onstage after other people who've done rape jokes, and that's how I had to cut my teeth: Make a group of people who've just laughed at a rape joke laugh" (Marchese). In a study of club comedy from the perspective of female comics, Stephanie Brown heard similar observations. As she puts it, "womxn learn to put on a smile in the face of a barrage of sexist, racist, homophobic, or otherwise offensive jokes, especially at open mics where comics aren't screened . . . while generally not targeted at a specific person, offensive humor is a signal to marginalized comics that they aren't welcome in these spaces" (Brown 57). That unwelcome environment is the problem.

Of course, it is important to remember that there is nothing either inherently liberatory or restrictive about any particular artistic form. The restrictiveness comes in the particular ways it is practiced: the cultural norms and assumptions, the power structures baked into an industry, and the vested interests of that industry's gatekeepers. As countless theorists have documented, stand-up comedy is an arena that has been particularly hostile to minoritarian voices. As Michael Jeffries puts it, "people from nondominant groups must figure out how to present themselves and work in a labor market dominated by white men, who set standards and dole out rewards" (4). Krefting exhorts comedy scholars not to fetishize resistant comedy, when so much of it is not. Instead, as she explains, "scholarship can benefit from examining larger industry forces—comedy club bookers and managers, agents, network executives, advertising and social media—as networks of power that reproduce social inequalities and perpetuate masculinist comic traditions" ("Hannah Gadsby Stands Down" 170). However, none of this is to say that there is something deterministic about the stand-up form itself that makes it regressive. Though it does largely function this way, it need not be so.

Indeed, one of the major takeaways from *Nanette* is Gadsby's plea for the industry to change. In many ways, this chimed nicely with the reawakening of the #MeToo movement by celebrities who adapted the phrase from the Black feminist activist Tarana Burke, first by targeting Harvey Weinstein and then shaming other powerful men in the entertainment industry who had routinely abused that power. As Gadsby reports, "The point was to break comedy so I could rebuild it and reshape it, reform it into something that could better hold everything I needed to share, and that is what I meant when I said I quit comedy" ("Three Ideas"). In *Nanette*, Gadsby explicitly asks more of both the comedy industry and the larger culture that built that industry. As we've explored, Gadsby reports that they did not think the sentiment would be a particularly popular one. They relate, "I fully expected by breaking the contract of comedy and telling my story in all its truth and pain that that would push me further into the margins of both life and art" ("Three Ideas"). Instead, they found connection between them and a great many appreciative audience members.

By describing *Nanette* as a challenge to the comedy industry, I may sound as if I am speaking about a challenge to one little corner of the entertainment world, a niche issue of interest only to a select group of industry insiders. That could not be further from the truth. The enthusiasm from so many audience members was not about, say, sticking it to a handful of comedy titans. To many it felt like a full-scale cultural reckoning. In other words, by drawing attention to the long-standing canards about women's or lesbians' humorlessness, about who is allowed to be angry on stage, and about what parts of a story can be told, Gadsby opened up space for questioning the many underlying cultural assumptions about gender, sexuality, and power.

Nanette's Critical and Popular Reception

Judging by what we have observed in previous chapters around outspoken women who do not conform to gendered expectations, one would assume that after *Nanette* gained notoriety, it would also attract a great deal of vitriol and blowback. Indeed, Gadsby violates almost every unwritten rule for women in the public eye. They are undisguisedly feminist. They are outspoken. They do not obey the strictures of heterosexual beauty ideals. Perhaps most strikingly, as they themself point out, they are unapologetically angry. Indeed, they aim their anger, outspokenness, and feminist worldview at the male-dominated world of stand-up comedy, explicitly calling for change. This is generally a recipe for a full-scale deluge of trolling and harassment, but that is not the full story of what happened in this case.

There was some backlash but of a relatively tepid variety. As word of *Nanette* was spreading soon after its debut on Netflix, some complained that the rapturous recommendations about this new comedy special were misplaced, as it should not count as comedy. As Matthew Monagle describes, "scroll through Twitter or Reddit and you'll find plenty of people who are willing to admit that it's fine, it's just not really comedy; they would prefer we describe *Nanette* as an indie TED Talk or some kind of public speaking event due to the lack of conventional humor in the set." The most commonly repeated complaint is that the special should not be advertised as comedy. Of course, these comments ignore the fact that there are indeed plenty of jokes in *Nanette*, and the live audience at the taping laughs quite often. But Gadsby does craft the final section of the special to be almost entirely joke free. To be clear, that is not an example of failed humor. They do not tell jokes that fall flat; rather, they just stop telling any at all as they complete their searing conclusion. After describing the griping about their jokeless segments from mostly male commentators, Monagle goes on to say, "The cognitive dissonance in this should be obvious to most—men are rejecting an unconventional standup special because it takes men to task for rejecting anything that breaks with their idea of convention." Nevertheless, those sorts of complaints continued to surround *Nanette*. And, predictably, if one peruses the comments underneath the trailer for *Nanette* on YouTube, there are many commenters who repeat the complaint, adding a variety of insults for good measure. A number also accuse the special of being propaganda rather than comedy. This particular conclusion presumably stems from the commenters' assumption that the special has a feminist or queer agenda, which for some is the equivalent of propaganda.

However, there was such an outpouring of praise for the special, both through formal reviews and informal internet conversations, that it far overwhelmed the negative feedback in the popular press. Indeed, there were several waves of articles written about *Nanette*, beginning with excellent reviews, then fierce defenses of the piece in light of criticism, and then a variety of think pieces on what exactly the special meant to comedy, to women and LGBTQ people, to the #MeToo movement, and to the culture at large. Many established professional comedians tweeted out their awe and admiration for Gadsby, someone most had never heard of until that moment. Kathy Griffin tweeted of *Nanette*, "It will change your life" (Ryzik). A reporter for *USA Today* wrote, "She offers at once a deep indictment of stand-up comedy and a mastery of the form" (Lawler). As the *New York Times* reported, "Netflix does not release viewership data, but judging by its social media mentions, 'Nanette' is among its most-positively received specials ever, a spokeswoman said" (Ryzik). In interviews, Gadsby has expressed shock not simply at their meteoric rise to fame but at the relative lack of negative attacks. They explain, "Just being a female comic, I've been getting horrific stuff online for my whole career. Being a physical woman in comedy, you get that really hostile [feedback]. And I learned how to deal with that. I was really blown away by how little I got from *Nanette*. There's been a bit, but to scale it's been overwhelmingly positive" (Lancaster).

Besides the fact that *Nanette* is undoubtedly well written and well executed, part of its enormous impact can also be attributed to timing. When it debuted on Netflix in June 2018, the #MeToo movement was reaching a crescendo as, one after another, victims publicly broke their silence by accusing powerful, high-profile men of sexual misconduct. This movement greatly affected the cultural conversation around sexual assault and abuse of power as it demonstrated the near ubiquity of sexual harassment and provided compelling evidence that the long-standing silence around the topic had been serving to perpetuate the problem and to shore up a culture of impunity for male celebrities and power brokers in particular.

Though Gadsby had begun working on *Nanette* several years previously, when it was released on Netflix the audience had been newly primed to hear the critique they were making (some with renewed anger, some with less skepticism than in the past). Indeed, it appears there were many audience members out there who were itching for someone to articulate this kind of extended argument in a compelling manner. As a writer from the *New Yorker* put it, the show "seems to harness the broader fury of the #MeToo moment. Gadsby, like many women, is done hiding her anger, and in 'Nanette' she bends the bounds of standup to accommodate it" (Donegan). Authors both professional and amateur discussed their own personal feelings brought up by the show or spoke on behalf of constituencies such as women or queer people about how welcome Gadsby's message has been. For instance, one writer from *The Guardian* argues, "the fervent way *Nanette* has been received suggests as audiences we are tired of self-deprecation from female comics, from queer comics, from—as Gadsby calls herself—the 'not normal.' We want the artists like Gadsby to yell and relish and stake their place. When Gadsby punches out to break open a new space for herself, she manages to break open a new space for us all" (Howard).

There have been just a few dissenting critical voices. Soraya Roberts, for one, wrote a scathing article in *The Baffler* in which she accuses those praising *Nanette* of lauding it more for its social import than its artistry. She asserts, "When bad art is still heralded as good—or 'necessary'—because it represents the sort of diversity we currently crave and so rarely find, that is cultural tokenism. And cultural tokenism is the enemy of criticism" (Roberts). I would grant Roberts's observation that people's reactions to *Nanette* were overwhelmingly reactions to its activism. Indeed, giving the special a favorable review or telling one's friends about it were not simply recommendations about Gadsby's skills as a performer. Rather, they were also endorsements of Gadsby's message. The enthusiastic audience response implicitly contained chorus after chorus of "yes, we agree!" Fans did not simply remark that it was an excellent piece. They said things like, "If there's one perspective on the #MeToo movement that everyone needs to hear—for the sake of humanity, really—it's Gadsby's" (Bhatt). I would argue that consuming *Nanette* was at least partially about consuming its success, about being a part of it, and about cheering it on. In a sense, then, *Nanette* and Gadsby themself became a cultural node of identification. Public fandom of the special became a way of performing one's support for hearing more stories like theirs, for shaking up the comedy industry and stand-up genre, and by extension, the wider culture that built it.

However, contrary to Roberts, I don't think that negates its artistry. Gadsby was not the first to say many of the things they said. As discussed, sexual violence was all over the news. But their story resonated with audiences on a personal level far beyond what any of the news articles did. While the initial impetus for the #MeToo movement began with Harvey Weinstein and then moved systematically to shame other male power brokers, Gadsby focused attention on the everyday traumas of individuals. And their telling moved people, which I would posit as a useful barometer for the success of any form of art. In some ways, it also helped dislodge a catch in the wider discourse, as *Nanette* itself provided the impetus for a flurry of writing and cultural commentary on the topics they raised. In this case, the special set the agenda and provided an opening for the feminist and queer press to follow. And in the age of Twitter, a greater number of people were able to weigh in, creating a further groundswell of support for their framing of the issues.

The piece gave both journalists and amateur commentators license to write extended think pieces on sexual violence, toxic masculinity, and female rage, among others. In much of this writing, reporters articulated the impression that *Nanette* felt like the turning of a corner or the start of something new. Commenting on the way in which Gadsby makes use of the comedy "callback" (in which jokes refer back to others told earlier in the show), Moira Donegan refers to the #MeToo movement itself as a type of callback, "a collective return to stories that women have been telling one way—to others, to themselves— with a new, emboldened understanding that those past tellings had been inadequate. Like Gadsby, many women have excluded or elided the difficult parts of their stories for the sake of a punch line, the sake of not upsetting the status quo, or the sake of the comfort of their listeners." She implies that the

#MeToo movement has encouraged women to reevaluate and retell their own stories. *Nanette* further builds on that movement with Gadsby asserting that they must "find a way of communicating the traumatic narratives of her life that she had always edited out of her material" (Luckhurst 60).

More than anything, the special was treated as a fork in the road for the comedy industry. Commentators of all stripes picked up on the fact that *Nanette* offered a challenge to the comedy world in both form and content. Fellow lesbian-feminist comedian Tig Notaro noted that Gadsby had successfully disrupted the comedy industry. She wrote, "It's going to be very interesting to see what comedians do post-*Nanette* . . . she cleared the table for necessary regrowth" (Ryzik). The first element of this challenge to comedy entails pointing to the ongoing exclusions and biases in the art world (both in comedy and high art). In Gadsby's long discussion of Picasso, they explain that he was considered revolutionary because he freed us from single-point perspective with his development of cubism, which allows multiple viewpoints to be represented on the canvas at the same time. Gadsby sarcastically thanks him before posing a question: "Thank you, Picasso. What a guy. What a hero. Thank you. But tell me, any of those perspectives a woman's? No. Well, I'm not fucking interested." As Donegan explains, Gadsby makes clear that "[art]—from painting to comedy—does not liberate everyone equally. It can replicate the same privileges and exclusions as the culture in which it was made." In their repeated refrain that they will have to quit comedy, Gadsby moves from playfully suggesting that perhaps they themself are the problem to more and more pointedly demonstrating why it is the industry itself that is toxic for many.

The outpouring of support for the special and the effusive press it generated reminds us that we do need cultural touchstones in order to move the cultural conversation. While the sudden deluge of stories about powerful men who victimized the people (mostly women) around them shocked the world as the #MeToo movement gathered steam, works like *Nanette* provided an individual experience of trauma with which to sympathize, a dissection of cultural hypocrisies with which to laugh, and the righteous anger with which to identify.

Douglas

A little less than two years after *Nanette* debuted on Netflix, Gadsby released a second comedy special on the streaming platform in May 2020, titled *Douglas*. At this point, the comic was in a very different position, as they now had the acclaim for their previous work buoying them along, something they directly acknowledge at the opening of the new piece. Indeed, *Douglas* is, in many ways, Gadsby's response to the discourse surrounding *Nanette*. They confess that they had no plans of making it in America, but "then what happened though is I wrote a show called *Nanette*—" at which point they are interrupted by enthusiastic applause. Confirming that much of the audience is there because they were fans of *Nanette*, they pose the question, "If you're here because of *Nanette* . . . why? Like, don't get me wrong, it was a good show. Solid bit of work. I'm quite fond. But it was a particular show of a very particular flavor. And if that is what has brought [you] . . . what the fuck are you expecting from this show? Because I'm sorry, if it's more trauma, I . . . I am fresh out." Referring to *Douglas* as their "difficult second album," they acknowledge that expectations are now high. They explain that since they have no way of knowing what people are going to want out of this show, they are going to adjust everyone's expectations by thoroughly laying out exactly what is going to happen. Which is indeed what they do. They spend roughly a third of the show telling us what they are going to do in the show. It qualifies as precisely the sort of thing a comic would normally be told to avoid, but they succeed in doing it all in a very amusing way while seeding a number of future jokes and callbacks and without ruining any coming punchlines.

As they warn the audience when they quip that they are "out of trauma," *Douglas* is less raw and confessional than was *Nanette*. Nevertheless, it picks up and runs with many of the themes and driving preoccupations of the earlier work. As they explain in their overview, the show contains "a fair dose of what I call a gentle and very good-natured needling of the patriarchy." They follow this up with a warning that "it's very important that you expect that, because it is there, and if that's not your thing . . . Leave. I've given you plenty of warning. Just go. Off you pop, man-flakes. Out you go. Go on with you." Though they cover quite a range of topics, they do continually return to male power and ego—this includes the way in which men have named all the things (like an obscure part of the female body called the "pouch of Douglas"), the way male artists have historically depicted women, and their experience with a supremely condescending male doctor. The common theme linking many of these topics is the power men have always had to make the rules and define reality. At one point, they allude back to *Nanette* in their extended discussion of what to expect in the coming set by advising audience members that if they ever feel offended by one of their jokes, they should remember that they are just jokes. They explain, "Even if you find yourself surrounded by people who are laughing at something you find objectionable . . . just remember the golden rule of comedy, which is, if you're in a minority, you do not matter. You don't. Don't blame me. I didn't write the rules of comedy. Men did. Blame them. I do. It's cathartic." It is both a callback to their critique of the comedy industry in *Nanette* and a link to their newer theme about male rulemaking.

The other through line to *Nanette* is that Gadsby allows themself to luxuriate in their own anger in this show. Unlike in *Nanette*, in which their anger is linked to their experience of trauma—a raw and righteous anger—in *Douglas* they take us on a tour of their moments of irrational anger, just for the fun of it. They refer to their tendency to angrily swell up in response to small provocations as their "puffer-fish" moments. Many of the examples they give are quite humorous and silly, including their disproportionate anger at the concept of the paleo diet and their hatred of the cartoon franchise *Teenage Mutant Ninja Turtles*. While *Nanette* was a statement about the toxicity of comedy norms for women and minorities, including prohibitions against anger, *Douglas* allows Gadsby to happily step outside of those rules.

As they explain in an interview, they had built their career on jokes that were apologies for themself. They say, "It's what most people do. You have to explain who you are, and you point to a difference that you have. That's your angle. But when it becomes the only reason you speak, it becomes an issue; all your material revolves around why you're different. The great freedom post-'Nanette' was that I'd put all that on the table" (Marchese). In fact, *Douglas* is structured around the revelation that Gadsby is on the autism spectrum (something that they had only discovered about themself fairly recently). This information is not given to the audience in order to wring humor from their weirdness; rather, they depict the syndrome as the source of their unique perspective on the world, a perspective that fuels their gift for comedy. Admitting that being on the autism spectrum can be frustrating and lonely, they assert that nevertheless they like the way they think, explaining, "If the world is right and I'm right in it, I can find my funny zip and my thinking expands. There is beauty in the way that I think."

Gadsby also happily taunts their "haters" throughout *Douglas*, joking about their enjoyment of "snacking on the hate." In other words, rather than being intimidated by previous critique or harassment, they thumb their nose at it. Explaining that there were some men who got very upset about *Nanette* not being funny enough, they state that it does not bother them, as they "still have the loud stick." But they marvel over the fact that they continue to get messages from men who just need to tell them, in all caps, that they have never heard of them. They go on, "I can't experience the humiliation I know they're so desperate for me to feel because I can't help but feel worried for them. Because that's a tough life. If new things are so painful . . . Ow. They . . . That's a learning difficulty. Imagine school for someone like that. Long division. 'I've never fucking heard of it!!!'" It is a funny bit, while it also functions similarly to Samantha Bee's "web extras" material (discussed in chapter 4), designed to draw attention to the harassment outspoken women receive while simultaneously disarming that harassment by rendering it laughable.

Expectations

Douglas was generally well received by both fans and critics. The reviews, though not quite as rapturous as those for *Nanette*, were almost universally positive (with a few exceptions). Gadsby was praised both for crafting a very funny, cleverly constructed show and for offering further inspiration. As Patrick Gomez of the *AV Club* put it, "*Douglas* is about reestablishing trust under Gadsby's new terms. And she delivers on everything she promises." The majority of reviewers seemed to agree that Gadsby is a formidable talent who is continuing to remake the comedy industry.

That said, there were more caveats and notes of wistfulness in a few of the reviews. For some on the political left, there seemed to be a longing for something more. The general through line of these responses was a desire for a more fully fleshed-out, nuanced critique of inequality and power. A reviewer for *Now Magazine*, for instance, remarked that some of the anti-male material struck her as "border-line essentialist" (Cole). Another reviewer notes that Gadsby does not satisfactorily interrogate their own forms of privilege as a white woman, remarking that she wished Gadsby "could take the brilliant surrealism of her sleight of hand jokes, and apply this same surprising, questioning nuance to the way that she highlights structural inequality" (Hunt). In an overwhelmingly negative review, Hilton Als of the *New Yorker* (who reviewed the stage version of the show) explains that he felt alienated from the piece as a Black gay male critic, as he thought that their sword-wielding at their male critics lacked nuance. He accuses them of espousing "a kind of puritan-minded radicalism in which someone else is always to blame for how messed up she feels. But isn't that messed-up feeling life? And what about other lives? What about the millions who have it worse, who are fighting to survive? On Gadsby's stage, solipsism masquerades as art."

It is certainly fair to point out that Gadsby's comedic analysis of social ills is far sharper when it comes to gender than it is on race or class. In fact, they rarely touch on either. Indeed, as Jack Halberstam points out, their discussion in *Nanette* of the difficulty of growing up in homophobic 1970s and '80s Tasmania does not even tangentially allude to the brutally violent colonialist history of how modern Tasmania was formed, a history from which all white Tasmanians benefited and which also created the particular form of virulent homophobia and toxic white masculinity to which Gadsby is reacting. However, as Halberstam also gestures to, all comedy is written from a particular positionality (not from a universal perch on high), and Gadsby's position, as a butch lesbian (particularly a neurodiverse one) is still incredibly rare in mainstream comedy. As Halberstam puts it, "she takes a white man's art and uses it magically to deconstruct the genre and in the process to remake it." I would argue that it is because such a perspective is still so rare that there is a strong desire for it to do everything. Because *Nanette* was seen as communicating an important and urgent message (one that became all the more amplified due to its unanticipated success), Gadsby became something of a public intellectual almost overnight, with all the raised expectations that entails.

Prior to the proliferation of cable networks and the development of narrowcasting (beginning roughly in the 1990s), we rarely looked to popular cultural entertainers and comedians for political or cultural analysis. But with the proliferation of more specialized content came what Geoffrey Baym refers to as "discursive integration," in that "discourses of news, politics, entertainment, and marketing have grown deeply inseparable; the languages and practices of each have lost their distinctiveness and are being melded into previously unimagined combinations" (262). Part of that melding produced television programs, such as *The Daily Show* and *The Colbert Report* (in the early 2000s), that provided sustained comedic dissections of mainstream political discourse. As I've discussed at length elsewhere (Day 76–83), the popularity of these programs quickly established their hosts, not simply as popular entertainers, but as knowledgeable political pundits in their own right. Fans looked to them not just for comedy but for providing the witty takedowns of political hypocrisies that they craved. In some senses, they were positioned both as the audience's stand-ins and as the spokespeople for a particular brand of left-leaning, informed critique of the failings of mainstream political debate.

Similarly, as the woman who publicly called out the misogyny and homophobia embedded in the comedy industry, in Western art, and in contemporary culture, while also poignantly revealing their own resulting trauma, Gadsby spoke truths that many fans had been longing to hear. Thus, they became a de facto figurehead, someone with the ability to bring a progressive critique of gender, sexuality, and power into mainstream conversation. But, of course, in many ways that is an impossibly high bar to continue to meet. Since they are a smart analyst, fans are now craving an almost academic-level evaluation of culture while also making us laugh. Others would like them to represent their positionality in particular. They are looked to as a spokesperson in a way that we do not ask of most comedians. Again, this is largely due to the fact that they are one of the only performers who has registered at the broad, popular culture level, who is offering a "gender not normal" analysis in their work. It is an analysis that many are clearly hungry to hear articulated. While we have seen many examples of the political Right attempting to hold the discursive line on gendered norms and expectations, the political Left is similarly interested in positioning comedy as always politically progressive and socially transgressive.

Conclusion

Krefting has argued that audiences' historic "lack of enthusiasm for women comic performers is symptomatic of power differentials" as "there is no economic or cultural incentive for buying into women's perspectives, particularly when they draw attention to their status as marginalized by producing charged humor" (*All Joking Aside* 110). As she explains, humor coming from "women and members of minority communities that falls flat with audience members can reflect a culture's lack of desire to acknowledge the experiences of the Other, signaling their tacit exclusion from the national imagination" (122). As discussed, there is absolutely a vocal faction who have objected to calling *Nanette* comedy. While it would be unwise to make assumptions about what *all* of these objectors are thinking, it seems clear from the tenor of comments found on discussion boards and the like that this unwillingness to acknowledge the experiences of the Other almost certainly plays into the more pointed rejections of the piece. That said, it also raises the question whether the unexpected embrace of *Nanette* by so many other audience members possibly signals a broader cultural shift. While many are actively disinterested in the experience of the Other, a substantial group are quite eager to bring the experiences of those Others into the mainstream. To be clear, I would certainly not argue that *Nanette* has somehow leveled the playing field for women or queer comics (let alone for women and queer citizens). However, it does appear to be symptomatic of a widening of the range of perspectives and subject positions with which mainstream audiences are willing to sympathize, as well as of an interest in challenging some of the old expectations around gendered norms.

As I have argued throughout this volume, it is no fluke that it was an outspoken feminist comedian who generated so much cultural conversation, reflection, and enthusiasm. Within the ongoing discursive contestation around gender, sexuality, and power, feminist comedians loom large for those on all sides of the battle lines. While there is certainly no end in sight to that war, Gadsby did advance their framing of the issues deeper into the mainstream than any one single performer usually does. Due to a combination of timing and talent, *Nanette* provided the opening for a number of brewing cultural critiques to emerge into the mainstream. This time, the engine driving those conversations were not predominantly the trolls or the outraged establishment. Instead, a combination of journalists, public figures, and citizen bloggers jumped into the fray to help move the public discourse. Indeed, it demonstrates that when a genre begins to transform, it is often through a combination of shifting cultural attitudes at large in concert with individual actors who become vectors for those changing attitudes. The new scenes of reception provided by social media help further amplify the reach of those individual actors if the timing is right. By latching on to this one text, singing its praises, recommending it to friends, or using it to speak about one's own life, many audience members implicitly (or explicitly) endorsed reevaluating the norms around both the comedy industry and public life. As this comedy special became a phenomenon, Gadsby seemed to provide hope that we could at last reframe some of our conversations around trauma, marginalization, gender, and power. As I discuss in the conclusion, that feeling of hope is not the only emotion that has continued to circle around Gadsby as their career has progressed post *Nanette*, but it was an extremely important one following the release of that special.

6

Conclusion

Female Comedians and the Cultural Imaginary

In writing this book, I have worked to draw attention to the way in which feminist comedians so often become the battleground on which cultural skirmishes are waged. These comedians, as a matter of course, regularly transgress social boundaries and expectations. In so doing, they elicit heightened emotional responses from audience members, emotional responses that periodically explode into moments of cultural controversy and debate. In these moments, we can see the public working through those boundaries, norms, and ideals, as varied constituencies fight to gain the conversational ball or to be the ones to frame the issues for everyone else. As we have seen, the individual comics themselves often have little control over the cultural discourse that circulates around their work in these individual moments of controversy, though they can and do position themselves to continue pushing against those cultural boundaries and to continue challenging expectations. As most comedians do, they strive to provide witty critique on the issues and obsessions of the day, occasionally managing to strike a nerve. That said, none of the performers profiled in this volume exist solely (or even mostly) within a permanent state of controversy and public attention (though neither have any of them disappeared from public life). Rather, since each of the controversies highlighted in previous chapters, each comedian has experienced professional ebbs and flows.

Interestingly, if we examine these women's careers since their most heightened moments of public scrutiny thus far, the person who has attracted the least subsequent controversy or debate has been Leslie Jones. Though we began the book with the shockingly nasty and focused attacks directed at Jones, attacks that allowed the manosphere to gain an elevated public presence, since emotions around the *Ghostbusters* reboot have faded away, so too has the target painted on Jones in particular. This is likely because she is arguably the least overtly political or stridently feminist of the performers, and once the manosphere had kicked up a fuss about *Ghostbusters*, they were relatively uninterested in Jones's career. After leaving *Saturday Night Live*, Jones has served as a commentator on the Olympic Games, hosted a game show, guest hosted *The Daily Show*, and cameoed in a variety of comedic films and television series. She also wrote a memoir published in 2023 about her life as a performer that was very well received. Four months after it was released, the book had several thousand reviews on both Amazon and Goodreads, at least 80 percent of which were four stars or above. Even the less favorable reviews did not appear to have been authored by trolls or others intent on deliberately sinking the ratings. No one on these sites seems particularly upset by her post *Ghostbusters* success as a comic. Rather, readers overwhelmingly attest to enjoying her comedy. At the end of her memoir, though, Jones mentions her increasing interest in politics (L. Jones 259–61). I have no doubt that if that interest begins to affect the sorts of projects she takes on, she could once again find herself at the center of cultural division.

As for Amy Schumer, after her whirlwind ride to fame (and scrutiny from all quarters), she had a period of lower-profile work. In 2019, she did a stand-up tour while experiencing a very difficult pregnancy marked by hyperemesis (which causes extreme forms of nausea and vomiting). While subsequently caring for a newborn and weathering the COVID pandemic, Schumer was in a reality cooking show with her chef husband and a documentary series about her challenging pregnancy. As a writer with *Rolling Stone* noted, "she hardly vanished, yet she wasn't as present in the zeitgeist as she had been in the Comedy Central days" (Sepinwall). She returned to more high-profile work in 2022, debuting a fictionalized program about her life called *Life and Beth* and rebooting her long-dormant sketch series *Inside Amy Schumer* (*IAS*) for another season. Critical reviews for *Life and Beth* were strong, while those for *IAS*'s fifth season were mediocre to good. Online user reviews for the two different series, though, were starkly divergent in tone. If one peruses Rotten Tomatoes or Google user reviews for *Life and Beth*, one finds a mix of generally well-considered appraisals of the program, some concluding that it is boring or complaining that the character is unlikeable, but many more expressing admiration and enthusiasm for the show or praising its relatability. In other words, they feel like genuine reviews. Those for *Inside Amy Schumer*, however, look overwhelmingly like they did near the end of *IAS*'s original run. On Google, there are long strings of one-star reviews piling up on one another that do not actually appraise the merit of the program but instead take aim at Amy Schumer's appearance, accuse her of stealing jokes, string together ad hominem insults, or falsely report that Schumer has admitted to committing sexual assault. In other words, they stem from that familiar policing of Schumer's transgressions (of beauty norms, propriety, gender roles, and comedy industry norms). It is curious that *Life and Beth* did not elicit the same defensive emotions, but this is perhaps explained by the fact that the program is more of a dramedy (somewhat outside of the more heavily policed worlds of stand-up or sketch comedy) and that *IAS* was already a recognizable program that antifans were primed to take notice of when it returned.

While these reviews were not necessarily newsworthy, the ire directed at Schumer did make headlines a year later after she had spoken publicly on geopolitical events. In the fall of 2023, following the Hamas-led attacks in Israel, Schumer repeatedly posted on social media in support of Israelis and against brewing antisemitic attacks. As we know, the public conversation around the attacks and the ensuing siege of Gaza was undoubtedly contentious and uncivil all around, but once again, Schumer became a particularly visible lightning rod for outrage. She temporarily shut down comments on her Instagram page after receiving a torrent of abuse, some of it related to the war or accusations of Islamophobia, with much of it again mixed up in insults about her looks, her privilege, and some new vaguely antisemitic insinuations that she was part of a conspiracy involving her distant cousin Senator Chuck Schumer. Some of this abuse caught public notice because a minor political figure became implicated; a staffer for Los Angeles city councilmember Hugo Soto-Martinez resigned when he was outed for some particularly offensive comments about Schumer on Twitter. The account for a podcast called TrueAnon began a thread about Schumer (and her previous statements about family members who had suffered during the Holocaust) by quipping, "The nazis named a concentration camp after her. It was called Da Cow" (Hays). According to Fox News, the staffer replied to the thread with "it's f—— up that you would say this about her when you know it was actually Cowschwitz" (Hays). Again, it is difficult to find reasoned and respectful discourse on the Israel-Palestine war on Twitter, but the conversation around Schumer is inevitably tainted by the loathing that she elicits from antifans, especially when she is vocal about her opinions. As the ups and downs of her career attest, I would wager that she is likely to have continued professional success in the future (despite the intensity of her critics, she has many more fans), while her work and her persona are equally likely to continue attracting concentrated opprobrium, particularly if she maintains her outspoken and unapologetic outlook.

In following up on the careers of Samantha Bee and Michelle Wolf, the first thing to note is that neither are in possession of their respective late-night programs anymore. Michelle Wolf's (*The Break with Michelle Wolf*) premiered on Netflix shortly after her appearance at the White House Correspondents' Association dinner, but it lasted only three months before Netflix pulled the plug. This was possibly due to poor ratings, though Netflix does not reveal viewership data. Alternatively, it could have been because Wolf's material was more controversial than Netflix was willing to support—for instance, she did a segment on her Fourth of July episode called "Salute to Abortions" (*The Break*, July 4, 2018). Samantha Bee's program *Full Frontal with Samantha Bee* lasted far longer on TBS, running from 2016 until 2022 (four years beyond the Ivanka Trump incident). However, after TBS's parent company merged with another, it axed several of its existing comedy programs, including *Full Frontal*, which had fallen in ratings. Following the cancellation of these shows, neither comedian has disappeared. Michelle Wolf has released several well-received stand-up comedy specials and was also invited to guest host *The Daily Show*. Her star has continued to rise in the stand-up comedy world. As discussed, streaming giant Netflix has helped proliferate stand-up comedy specials, carrying a wide variety of performers who appeal to vastly divergent taste cultures. There, Wolf has been able to carve out her own niche of very funny and forthright comedy that pulls no punches, and provided that something she has said does not get noticed within broader circles, she will likely avoid the type of widespread controversy that followed her White House Correspondents' Dinner performance. Samantha Bee, on the other hand, has not gone away but has had less high-profile work since her show's cancellation. She embarked on a live tour and continued to host a podcast. At the time of writing, she was reportedly at work on a children's sketch comedy program. I would say, though, that, in the near future, it is unlikely that she will again have as prominent an outlet as *Full Frontal*. Both Bee and Wolf now have reputations as opinionated feminist comedians who don't shy away from controversy. That may not inhibit Wolf's abilities to produce more stand-up specials, particularly now that she is quite recognizable, but it will be a harder sell for Bee if she continues to work in the more mainstream world of network television.

Interestingly, the performer in this volume who first experienced the most overwhelmingly positive cultural buzz, Hannah Gadsby, is the one who has also subsequently experienced the most backlash. As discussed in chapter 5, after *Nanette*, Gadsby's second Netflix special was called *Douglas*. In 2023, they released their third, called *Something Special*, which was again critically well received, though also far less widely discussed than the one-of-a-kind *Nanette*. But it was their brief foray into another medium later that year that again bumped them back to the center of cultural conversations. In the summer of 2023, an art exhibit ran at the Brooklyn Museum that Gadsby cocurated called *It's Pablo-matic: Picasso According to Hannah Gadsby*. The exhibit was one of many around the word that was timed to coincide with the fiftieth anniversary of Pablo Picasso's death, only this one was centered on Gadsby's critique of Picasso, which they had begun in *Nanette*. The museum's publicity materials describe the show as examining "the artist's complicated legacy through a critical, contemporary, and feminist lens, even as it acknowledges his work's transformative power and lasting influence" (Brooklyn Museum). Gadsby, who majored in art history in university, has long peppered critiques of Western art into their comedic commentary on gender and culture. They also memorably singled out Pablo Picasso for his misogyny in *Nanette*, which is presumably why the museum approached them to create a show that would use this critique as a jumping off point. But as soon as the show was announced, the derisive anticipation began building. As a reviewer for *Artnet* put it, in stark contrast to the critical celebration of *Nanette*, "I've never seen more critical backlash *in advance* than there has been for 'It's Pablo-matic.' . . . for months, every time I logged onto Twitter, someone from a different corner of the art commentary world would be snarking about it" (Davis). Then, once the show opened, a series of spectacularly nasty reviews rolled in.

Jason Farago's review in the *New York Times* was one of the most visible and also most gleefully condescending. Farago began by announcing that he found the show's title so silly that he had to cut and paste rather than type it into the review himself. Next, he attests to finding Gadsby's commentary/jokes that accompany the paintings off-puttingly adolescent due to their reliance on bodily humor. He then goes on to reveal what appears to be a simmering resentment over much of the content of *Nanette*, particularly the fact that it contained art critique coming from a "comedian with moderate art historical bona fides," which he thought gave Gadsby's audience permission to believe that avant-garde painting was all a big scam. In particular, he refers several times to Gadsby's advocacy for the importance of telling everyone's stories, arguing "not long ago, it would have been embarrassing for adults to admit that they found avant-garde painting too difficult and preferred the comforts of story time" (Farago). After asserting that the feminist artists who were included in the show were not represented as fully as they could have been, he finally concludes with one last flourish that "the function of a public museum (or at least it should be) is to present to all of us these women's full aesthetic achievements; there is also room for story hour, in the children's wing" (Farago).

Of course, there are plenty of legitimate critiques that can be made about any art exhibit, including this one. Some of the critiques marshaled were undoubtedly well reasoned. However, the relish with which many of the critics took to eviscerating the show and to diminishing Gadsby in particular seemed disproportionate to the offenses. Though these were mainstream reviews, not ad hominem attacks made by avowed members of the manosphere (most of whom are presumably unlikely to attend an art exhibit in Brooklyn), they nevertheless seemed to originate from a well of long-standing antipathy and anger. And these reviews were of course then posted across Reddit forums and the like, which generated a great deal of schadenfreude among other posters, ushering in some of those ad hominem attacks. This resentment of Gadsby appeared to stem from some combination of wanting to take the comedian who dared to fancy themself an art historian down a peg and a related desire to make ridiculous the woke lesbian who had made people uncomfortable. Combined with all of that, the exhibit itself was, in some ways, a mash-up of genres, mixing comedy (Gadsby's quips beside particular paintings as well as their commentary in an accompanying audio guide) with an art exhibit. One could argue that it was an unsuccessful mash-up (though that is ultimately a matter of opinion), but as with *Nanette* itself, the very idea of challenging genre conventions is clearly upsetting to some viewers (Farago, for one, did not appreciate jokes about sphincters on an art gallery wall). Once again, Gadsby was the interloper who was happily transgressing boundaries around generic norms, gender roles, and historic precedent. Only this time, they did not have a wave of popular frustrations buoying them along. As I argue in the previous chapter, in addition to Gadsby's very real skills, part of the reason that

Nanette became not just a successful comedy special but a cultural sensation was that it hit the moment precisely, putting into words (pithy, heartfelt words at that) what many people had been longing to hear articulated, providing something tangible that people could identify with and publicly champion. At the time, the antifans were effectively drowned out by the chorus of other voices expressing their appreciation. That was not so for the Picasso exhibit, a medium in which many of Gadsby's fans are likely less comfortable. Those who had disliked *Nanette* or Gadsby in general could smell the blood in the water before this experimental exhibit had even opened, and these were the voices that dominated, despite there being a sizable minority of reviewers (both professional and amateur) who enjoyed and appreciated the exhibition.

While one could argue that the reaction to *It's Pablo-matic* belies my optimistic framing of the chapter on *Nanette* around the concept of "hope," I ultimately don't think it does. As discussed, the performers profiled in this volume, like other new voices to the comedy world, are opening up new spaces and new possibilities within popular culture. As a corollary, they are also attracting blowback; there are expanded opportunities for change, and there are angry roadblocks. Indeed, as I have argued, the work of feminist comedians is a site of constant discursive struggle, and in that struggle, there will inevitably be pushes and pulls by different constituencies, all seeking to shape the conversation. We see these battles at their most raw around feminist comedians because of all the ways in which they are transgressing boundaries. By simply existing in mainstream comedy they are already trespassing into traditionally male territory. By speaking forcefully, or politically, or about taboo topics, they are breaking long-held rules. The women profiled in this volume transgress industry standards, genre forms, gender norms, and speech conventions. Because they are doing so in the public eye, as part of popular culture, we intuit that the stakes are high. All of it is important to creating, re-creating, and challenging assumptions about gender and race, expectations for the way the world works, and understandings of what comedy is and how it is done.

While popular culture is frequently dismissed as frivolous and inconsequential to public and political life, it is ultimately the primary arena for battles over shaping public opinion. Cultural and political shifts do not come out of nowhere. They are worked out incrementally within popular culture amid ongoing discursive struggle over definitions, norms, and ideals. As discussed, comedy (writ large) is one of the hottest sites of this discursive strife, particularly as some of the more rigid old structures have come down and individuals have rushed to either defend the old norms or to disrupt them. And feminist comedy is one of the most combustible sites of all. As our case studies have demonstrated, many of the flashpoints of the contemporary culture wars swirl around feminist comics, whether that is the comic's intention or not. These culture war disputes are not a distraction from real-world politics and power. Rather, they are themselves skirmishes over the allocation of resources and the replication of power structures. They delineate the battle lines around which to fight for legislative change, cultural priorities, and status. They are also a much more accessible arena for average citizens than is electoral politics.

Though there is a constant push and pull of discursive contestation within popular culture, at various moments, some voices and perspectives become louder. This is one of the reasons why one cannot underestimate the power of radical groups like the alt-right or the manosphere. While these movements are undoubtedly populated by extremists, it would be folly to dismiss their power. Though the sentiments expressed might seem fringe or sometimes even laughably absurd, as we have seen, they have frequently been very successful in driving the public conversation. The grievances that are nurtured in niche chat rooms then spill out into the more central public sphere of online comment sections and then to journalistic reportage. Even when these reports are dismissed by much of the public, they have already often helped set the terms of the debate. As Dana Showalter, Shannon Stevens, and Daniel L. Horvath put it, the manosphere "does not pre-exist its own expression" (180); rather, it is continually re-created in circulated discourse about the inadequacy of female comedians, about movie reboots that desecrate a nostalgic original, and about men being disrespected by popular culture. It is created both by the polite online conversations and reviews and the vitriolic ones. Indeed, the more extreme voices are often an amplified version of the more mainstream ones, each tag-teaming the other on how to view particular texts, how to frame individual issues, and how to make sense of our world.

That said, artists' voices have the ability to do this as well. The example of Gadsby's *Nanette* demonstrates that a well-timed piece of art can work to set the agenda itself. Comedy in particular is especially adept at opening up new spaces and creating new frames, sometimes working to dislodge stuck bits of discourse, nudging the discussion in new directions. In Gadsby's case, they gave voice to some of the central simmering concerns of the #MeToo movement that had yet to be fully fleshed out in the mainstream, speaking truths that many longed to hear. We often need voices like these to help channel our conversations. From time to time, when a particular work strikes the right notes, it can become a cultural touchstone, helping focus the public debate. While there are few people in the general population motivated enough to go toe to toe with the alt-right trolls on comment pages online, many will eagerly rally around a popular cultural text that impacted them, helping spread and amplify the perspective articulated in that text.

Sometimes the way that performers become conduits is somewhat beyond their control. We see this, for instance, in the way that Amy Schumer has for many become the face of white feminism and its perceived flaws, despite not being the most doctrinaire feminist nor the most egregious of entitled white women. Her work is met with far more scrutiny and heightened affective responses than that of the average comic or actor. Indeed, all of the comedians profiled in this volume have had strong feelings projected onto them. In the varied responses to their work, we see an outsize amount of revulsion, loathing, and hatred as well as delight and hope.

Feminist comedy elicits such intense emotional states because gender is still such contested territory, while feminism is itself such a fraught, ever-shifting, culturally loaded conception. Funny, outspoken women are still transgressive and threatening to the status quo while also thrilling for those interested in challenging gendered norms. That frisson creates controversy, as the culture works out its divisions in and through the work of these performers. Those controversies are often not pretty. They can be brutal for both performer and fans, but they may indeed be necessary, as they provide the opportunity for varied belief systems and value structures to battle for public favor.

Looking toward the future, and to a new generation of feminist comedians who may attract similar controversy, discussion, and intense emotions, I would wager that we are going to see more trans comedians in this space. As I mention in the introduction, there are plenty of trans performers working currently, but none have yet achieved the type of culturally visible, mainstream success that would attract the kind of popular cultural controversies and moments of intense focus that are chronicled in this volume. However, in recent years, trans people have suddenly found themselves at the center of the culture wars, as greater visibility has coincided with increasingly targeted bathroom bills, regulations against medical treatment for trans youth, and general demonization by politicians intent on scoring easy political points with their constituencies. I have no doubt that trans comedians, who transgress all of the cultural boundaries around gender and comedy as do cisgendered female performers, could cut incisively through the morass in a way that captures public attention (and dismay).

One increasing trend that is pushing toward the development of such careers while also potentially inhibiting widespread discussion are the ever-more targeted forms of social media that comedians are using to find their audiences. Platforms like Slack or Patreon are facilitating the development of incredibly specialized micro-communities. On the one hand, this is undeniably a boon for experimental comedy, as it provides the opportunity for comedians to develop material that a broader audience might find radical, provocative, or simply incomprehensible, as the comedian can speak almost entirely to sympathetic listeners. Importantly, it also bypasses almost all of the traditional gatekeepers who have historically kept so many out of the comedy industry, whether because of gender, race, age, disability, and more. Indeed, this is one way of tackling many of the stubborn inequities in the comedy world. Specialized experimental comedy will also presumably invite less targeted trolling and fewer comedic controversies. On the flip side, that also means that it is likely to have less impact on the wider culture. Various types of online experimental comedy will (and do) exist in happy bubbles right next door to the happy white supremacist bubbles. I would not be the first to point out that a shrinking central public sphere is ultimately not good news for the democratic project; that applies not just to the higher-brow venues for debate but also for comedy and popular culture. I do hope that we continue to have performers who span multiple taste cultures and publics or who simply attract attention and controversy beyond a select fan base. The more high-profile material chronicled in this volume is where we find the fireworks. It is where some of the discrete cultural bubbles intersect and vie for favor in the popular imagination.

Since none of the inequities and divisions around gender have entirely withered away, neither have the points of friction, controversy, and debate. And so long as there are societal barriers, so too is there great potential power (as well as danger) in transgressing those barriers. Ultimately, if we want to continue tearing down the old walls around gender roles, we will look to the feminist comedians to do much of the cultural labor.

WORKS CITED

Aarons, Debra, and Marc Mierowsky. "The Marvelous Mrs. Maisel as an Alternative History of Stand-up." *Comedy Studies*, vol. 12, no. 1, 2021, pp. 46–64.

Abad-Santos, Alex. "Amy Schumer's Alleged Joke Stealing, Explained." *Vox*, 27 Jan. 2016.

———. "Marc Maron Stands Up for Amy Schumer: 'This Isn't about Justice, It's about Hate.'" *Vox*, 30 Jan. 2016.

Ahmed, Sara. *The Promise of Happiness*. Duke University Press, 2010.

Als, Hilton. "Hannah Gadsby's Song of the Self." *New Yorker*, 22 Jul. 2019, https://www.newyorker.com/magazine/2019/07/29/hannah-gadsbys-song-of-the-self.

Antoine, Katja. "'Pushing the Edge' of Race and Gender Hegemonies through Stand-up Comedy: Performing Slavery as Anti-Racist Critique." *Etnofoor*, vol. 28, no. 1, 2016, pp. 35–54.

Bailey, Moya. *Misogynoir Transformed: Women's Digital Resistance*. New York University Press, 2021.

Bakhtin, Mikhail. *Rabelais and His World*, translated by Helene Iswolsky, Indiana University Press, 1965.

Banet-Weiser, Sarah. *Empowered: Popular Feminism and Popular Misogyny*. Duke University Press, 2018.

Baym, Geoffrey. "*The Daily Show*: Discursive Integration and the Reinvention of Political Journalism." *Political Communication*, vol. 22, no. 3, 2005, pp. 259–76.

Bee, Samantha [@iamsambee]. "BETTER." *Twitter*, 14 Sep. 2015, https://twitter.com/iamsambee/status/643476935172038656?ref_src=twsrc%5Etfw%7Ctwcamp%5Etweetembed%7Ctwterm%5E643476935172038656%7Ctwgr%5E9791d7b8b2 6bee50befac1c69962f805bab9be6f%7Ctwcon%5Es1_&ref_url=https%3A%2F%2Fuproxx.com%2Ftv%2Fsamantha-bee-turned-late-night-ladies-into-centaurs%2F.

Bemiller, Michelle, and Rachel Zimmer Schneider. "It's Not Just a Joke." *Sociological Spectrum*, vol. 30, no. 4, 2010, pp. 459–79.

Bennett, Jessica. "About Samantha Bee, Ivanka Trump, and that Word." *New York Times*, 2 Jun. 2018, https://www.nytimes.com/2018/06/02/arts/television /samantha-bee-ivanka-trump.html.

Berman, Eliza. "Amy Schumer Knows She'll Make More Mistakes. But She Is Ready to Listen and Learn." *Time Magazine*, 12 Apr. 2018.

Bhatt, Neha. "Hannah Gadsby's 'Nanette': Comedic Catharsis." *MINT*, 6 Jul. 2018, https://www.livemint.com/Leisure/hNTEW8YuDtHBSgWMrycHFJ/Hannah -Gadsbys-Nanette-Comedic-catharsis.html.

Bradley, Laura. "Jon Stewart Doesn't Buy the Outrage about Samantha Bee's Ivanka Trump Dig." *Vanity Fair*, 4 Jun. 2018.

Brecht, Bertolt. *Brecht on Theatre: The Development of an Aesthetic*, edited and translated by John Willett, Eyre Methuen, 1964.

Brooklyn Museum. "It's Pablo-matic: Pablo Picasso According to Hannah Gadsby." Brooklynmuseum.org, Jun. 2–24, Sep. 2023.

Brown, Stephanie. "Open Mic? The Gendered Gatekeeping of Authenticity in Spaces of Live Stand-up Comedy." *Feminist Media Histories*, vol. 6, no. 4, 2022, pp. 42–67.

Bryan, Peter Cullen, and Brittany R. Clark. "#NotMyGhostbusters: Adaptation, Response, and Fan Entitlement in 2016's Ghostbusters." *The Journal of American Culture*, vol. 42, no. 2, Jun. 2019, pp. 147–58.

Brzezinski, Mika. "Watching a Wife and Mother . . ." *Twitter* Post, 29 Apr. 2018, https://twitter.com/morningmika/status/990585968825597954?lang=en.

Cole, Susan G. "TV Review: Hannah Gadsby's Follow-up to Netflix Hit Nanette Disappoints." *Now Magazine*, 26 May 2020.

Coletta, Lisa. "Postmodernity and the Gendered Uses of Political Satire." *Women and Comedy: History, Theory, and Practice*, edited by Peter Dickinson, Anne Higgins, Paul Matthew St. Pierre, Diana Solomon, and Sean Zwagerman, Fairleigh Dickinson University Press, 2014.

Collins, Patricia Hill. *From Black Power to Hip Hop: Racism, Nationalism, and Feminism*. Temple U Press, 2006.

Colpean, Michelle, and Meg Tully. "Not Just a Joke: Tina Fey, Amy Schumer, and the Weak Reflexivity of White Feminist Comedy." *Women's Studies in Communication*, vol. 42, no. 2, 2019, pp. 161–80.

Cook, Rebecca J., and Simone Cusack. *Gender Stereotypes: Transnational Legal Perspectives*. University of Philadelphia Press, 2010.

Dargis, Manohla. "Our 'Ghostbusters' Review: Girls Rule. Women are Funny. Get Over it." *New York Times*, 10 Jul. 2016.

Davis, Ben. "The Brooklyn Museum's Much Criticized 'It's Pablomatic' Show Is Actually Weirdly at War with Itself Over Hannah Gadsby's Art History." *Artnet*, 20 Jun. 2023.

Day, Amber. *Satire and Dissent: Interventions in Contemporary Political Debate*. Indiana University Press, 2011.

Donegan, Moira. "The Comedian forcing Standup to confront the #MeToo Era." *New Yorker*, 28 Jun. 2018, https://www.newyorker.com/culture/culture-desk/the-comedian-forcing-stand-up-to-confront-the-metoo-era.

Douglas, Mary. *Purity and Danger: Routledge Classics*. Routledge, 1966, 2002.

Finley, Karen. *A Different Kind of Intimacy: The Collected Writings of Karen Finley*. Thunder Mountain Press, 2000.

Farago, Jason. "With Hannah Gadsby's 'It's Pablo-matic,' the Joke's on the Brooklyn Museum." *New York Times*, 6 Jun. 2023.

Flynn, Meagan. "Trump Scolds 'Filthy' Comedian, Head of Correspondents Group Regrets Monologue." *Washington Post*, 30 Apr. 2018, https://www.washingtonpost.com/ news/morning-mix/wp/2018/04/30/trump-scolds-filthy-comedian -michelle-wolf/.

Fraser, Nancy. "Rethinking the Public Sphere: A Contribution to the Critique of Actually Existing Democracy." *Habermas and the Public Sphere*, edited by Craig Calhoun, MIT Press, 1992, pp. 109–42.

Fuentes Morgan, Danielle. *Laughing to Keep From Dying: African American Satire in the Twenty-First Century*. University of Illinois Press, 2020.

Full Frontal with Samantha Bee. "ICE Misplaces 1,500 Children." *TBS*, 23 May 2018.

———. "Missing Migrant Children Update." Episode 84. *TBS*, 6 Jun. 2018.

Gadsby, Hannah. *Nanette*. Netflix, 2018.

———. "Three Ideas. Three Contradictions. Or Not." *Ted Talk*, 2019.

Ghostbusters. Directed by Paul Feig, Columbia Pictures, 2016.

Gilbert, Joanne. *Performing Marginality: Humor, Gender, and Cultural Critique*. Wayne State University Press, 2004.

Gill, Rosalind. "Postfeminist Media Culture: Elements of a Sensibility." *European Journal of Cultural Studies*, vol. 10, no. 2, 2007, pp. 147–66.

Gilmore, Leigh, and Elizabeth Marshall. "Gender Pessimism and Survivor Storytelling in the Memoir Boom: Girl Interrupted, Autobiography of a Face, and Nanette." *Witnessing Girlhood: Towards an Intersectional Tradition of Life Writing*, edited by Leigh Gilmore and Elizabeth Marshall, Fordham University Press, 2019, pp. 38–62.

Goltz, Dustin Bradley. "Ironic Performativity: Amy Schumer's Big (White) Balls." *Text and Performance Quarterly*, vol. 35, no. 4, 2015, pp. 266–85.

Gomez, Patrick. "Hannah Gadsby Sets Realistic Expectations for *Nanette* Follow-up, *Douglas* – and then Exceeds them." *AV Club*, 26 May 2020.

Gray, Jonathan. "How Do I Dislike Thee? Let Me Count the Ways." *Antifandom: Dislike and Hate in the Digital Age*, edited by Melissa Click, New York University Press, 2019, pp. 25–41.

Gray, Jonathan, et al. *Satire TV: Politics and Comedy in the Post-Network Era*. New York University Press, 2009.

Greene, Viveca, and Amber Day. "Asking for It: Rape Myths, Satire, and Feminist Lacunae." *Signs: Journal of Women in Culture and Society*, vol. 45, no. 2, 2019, pp. 449–72.

Greene, Viveca. "'Deplorable' Satire: Alt-Right Memes, White Genocide Tweets, and Redpilling Normies." *Studies in American Humor*, vol. 5, no. 1, 2019, pp. 31–69.

———. "All They Need is Lulz: Racist Trolls, Unlaughter, and Leslie Jones." *The Joke is on Us: Political Comedy in (Late) Neoliberal Times*, edited by Julie A. Webber, Lexington Books, 2019.

Habermas, Jurgen. *The Structural Transformation of the Public Sphere: An Inquiry into a Category of Bourgeois Society*. Translated by Thomas Burger and Frederick Lawrence. MIT Press, 1989.

Hains, Tim. "Sarah Huckabee Sanders: Michelle Wolf Needs More 'Happiness' In Her Life." *Real Clear Politics*, 4 May 2018.

Halberstam, Jack. "Just Joking: Notes on the Comedy of Hannah Gadsby by Jack Halberstam." *Bullybloggers*, 9 Aug. 2019.

Hall, Stuart. "Notes on Deconstructing the Popular." *Cultural Resistance Reader*, edited by Stephen Duncombe, Verso, 2002, pp. 185–92.

Halperin, Julia. "Still Fighting Culture Wars: At Art Basel Miami Beach, Karen Finley Revisits One of Her Earlier Artworks." *New York Times*, 9 Dec. 2023, pp. C1, C6.

Hammerman, Shaina. "Dirty Jews: Amy Schumer and Other Vulgar Jewesses." *From Shtetl to Stardom: Jews in Hollywood*, edited by Michael Renov and Vincent Brook, Purdue University Press, 2017, pp. 49–72.

Harris, William. "The NEA Four: Life After Symbolhood." *New York Times*, 5 Jun. 1994.

Hashmi, Siraj. "Netflix Is Trashing Its Ratings System After Schumer Special Tanked." *Washington Examiner*, 17 Mar. 2017.

Hasson, Mary. "How Low Can Self-Hating Feminists Go? As Michelle Wolf Shows, Today's Feminism Is REPULSIVE To Women." *Daily Caller*, 8 May 2018, https://dailycaller.com/2018/05/08/self-hating-feminists-like-michelle-wolf-repulsive-to-women/.

Hays, Gabriel. "Aide to LA Councilmember Resigns after Making Antisemitic Jokes about Amy Schumer, Mayor Praises Exit." *Fox News*, 28 Oct. 2023.

Henley, Nancy, and Jo Freeman. "The Sexual Politics of Interpersonal Behavior." *Women: A Feminist Perspective*. 5th ed., edited by Jo Freeman, McGraw Hill, 1975, 1994.

Hennefeld, Maggie, et al. "In Focus: What's So Funny about Comedy and Humor Studies?" *Journal of Cinema and Media Studies*, vol. 58, no. 3, 2019, pp. 137–71.

Hennefeld, Maggie. "Abject Feminism, Grotesque Comedy, & Apocalyptic Laughter on *Inside Amy Schumer.*" *Abjection Incorporated: Mediating the Politics of Pleasure and Violence*, edited by Maggie Hennefeld and Nicholas Sammond, Duke University Press, 2020, pp. 86–111.

Hiesey, Monica. "Amy Schumer: Comedy's Viral Queen." *The Guardian*, 28 Jun. 2015.

Howard, Jane. "Hannah Gadsby's Nanette Dares to Dream of a Different Future – for Ourselves and for Comedy; The Simplicity of the Australian Standup's Netflix Special Gives us Space to Laugh and Cry, and Inspires us to Tell Our Own Stories." *The Guardian (London)*, 26 Jun. 2018, https://advance-lexis-com.bryant .idm.oclc.org/api/document?collection=news&id=urn:contentItem:5SN6 -CP21-JCJY-G1XM-00000-00&context=1516831.

Hunt, El. "'Hannah Gadsby: Douglas' Review: A Funny Yet Frustrating Encore from the 'Nanette' Comic." *New Musical Express*, 26 May 2020.

Jacobson, Murrey. "Dave Chapelle Says Wolf 'Nailed It' at White House Correspondents Dinner." *PBS.org*, 30 Aug. 2018.

Jane, Emma. "Hating 3.0: Should Anti-Fan Studies Be Renewed for Another Season?" *Antifandom: Dislike and Hate in the Digital Age*, edited by Melissa Click, New York University Press, 2019.

Jeffries, Michael P. *Behind the Laughs: Community and Inequality in Comedy*. Stanford University Press, 2017.

Jenkins, Nash. "Trump's Press Secretary Says Samantha Bee's Comment About Ivanka Trump Was Disgusting." *Time Magazine*, 31 May 2018, https://time .com/5297303/sarah-huckabee-sanders-ivanka-trump-samantha-bee/.

Jenzen, Olu. "A Queer Tension: The Difficult Comedy of Hannah Gadsby: Nanette." *Film Studies*, vol. 22, no. 1, May 2020, pp. 30–46.

Jones, Jeffrey P., and Geoffrey Baym. "A Dialogue on Satire News and the Crisis of Truth in Postmodern Political Television." *Journal of Communication Inquiry*, vol. 34, no. 3, 2010, pp. 278–94.

Jones, Leslie. *Leslie F*cking Jones: A Memoir*. Grand Central Press, 2023.

Jones, Van. *The Van Jones Show; Interview with Leslie Jones*. CNN, 11 Aug. 2018, https://advance-lexis-com.bryant.idm.oclc.org/api/document?collection=news &id=urn:contentItem:5T1J-DY41-DXH2-62VP-00000-00&context=1516831.

Kinnick, Katherine. "Media Morality Tales and the Politics of Motherhood." *Mommy Angst: Motherhood in America Popular Culture*, edited by Ann Hall and Mardia Bishop, Praeger, 2009.

Kohen, Yael. *We Killed: The Rise of Women in American Comedy*. Sarah Crichton Books, 2012.

Krefting, Rebecca. *All Joking Aside: American Humor and Its Discontents*. Johns Hopkins University Press, 2014.

———. "Hannah Gadsby Stands Down: Feminist Comedy Studies." *Journal of Cinema and Media Studies*, vol. 58, no. 3, 2019, pp. 165–70.

———. "Hannah Gadsby: On the Limits of Satire." *Studies in American Humor*, vol. 5, no. 1, 2019, pp. 93–102.

Kuipers, Giselinde. "The Politics of Humour in the Public Sphere: Cartoons, Power and Modernity in the First Transnational Humour Scandal." *European Journal of Cultural Studies*, vol. 14, no. 1, Mar. 2011, pp. 63–80.

Kumar, Sangeet. "The Fatal Snare of Proximity: Live Television, New Media, and the Witnessing of Mumbai Attacks." *South Asian History and Culture*, vol. 3, no. 4, 2012, pp. 532–48.

Lancaster, Brodie. "Hannah Gadsby: 'I'm Still Struggling with How Americans Make Tea'; The Acclaimed Comic Talks about Nanette's Legacy, Her Friendship with Emma Thompson, Louis CK's Comeback and How to Dress Like Her on Halloween." *The Guardian (London)*, 26 Oct. 2018, https://advance-lexis-com.bryant.idm.oclc.org/api/document?collection=news&id=urn:contentItem:5TK7-BDN1-JCJY-G17N-00000-00&context=1516831.

Landes, Joan B. *Women and the Public Sphere in the Age of the French Revolution*. Cornell University Press, 1988.

Lawler, Kelly. "Hannah Gadsby, Ali Wong and Michelle Wolf: Female Comedians Who Challenge Stand-up Comedy." *USA Today*, 17 Jul. 2018, https://www.usatoday.com/story/life/tv/2018/07/17/radical-female-comedians-hannah-gadsby-nanette-ali-wong-hard-knock-wife-michelle-wolf-break-netflix/776143002/.

Lawson, Caitlin E. "Platform Vulnerabilities: Harassment and Misogynoir in the Digital Attack on Leslie Jones." *Communication & Society*, vol. 21, no. 6, 2018, pp. 818–33.

Lennox, Mike Cidoni. "2018 Breakthrough: Hannah Gadsby May Change Stand-up Game." *AP News*, 14 Dec. 2018.

Lewis, Paul. *Cracking Up: American Humor in a Time of Conflict*. University of Chicago Press, 2006.

Lotz, Amanda. *The Television Will Be Revolutionized*. New York University Press, 2007.

Love, Matthew. "50 Best Stand-up Comics of All Time." *Rolling Stone*, 14 Feb. 2017.

Luckhurst, Mary. "Hannah Gadsby: Celebrity stand-up, Trauma, and the Meta-Theatrics of Persona Construction." *Persona Studies*, vol. 5, no. 2, pp. 53–66.

Madden, Stephanie, Melissa Janoske, Rowena Briones Winkler, and Amanda Nell Edgar. "Mediated Misogynoir: Intersecting Race and Gender in Online Harassment." *Mediating Misogyny: Gender, Technology, and Harassment*. Palgrave MacMillan, 2018.

Mahdawi, Arwa. "Is Lena Dunham's 'Hipster Racism' Just Old-Fashioned Preju-
    dice?" *The Guardian*, 25 Nov. 2017, https://www.theguardian.com/world/2017
    /nov/25/hipster-racism-lena-dunham-prejudice.

Mantilla, Karla. *Gendertrolling: How Misogyny Went Viral*. Praeger, 2015.

Marchese, David. "Hannah Gadsby on Comedy Trolls, Anti-Vaxxers and Burying Her
    Dog." *The New York Times*, 31 May 2020, https://www.nytimes.com/interactive
    /2020/05/25/magazine/hannah-gadsby-interview.html.

Marx, Nick. *Sketch Comedy: Identity, Reflexivity, and American Television*. Indiana
    University Press, 2019.

Meier, Matt. "Trump vs. Comedy: The Carnivalesque Politics of Late-Night." *Laugh-
    ter, Outrage, and Resistance: Post-Trump TV Satire in Political Discourse and Dissent*,
    edited by Lori Henson and Stacie Meihaus Jankowski, Peter Lang, 2020, pp. 7–26.

Mizejewski, Linda. *Pretty/Funny: Women Comedians and Body Politics*. University
    of Texas Press, 2014.

Mizejewski, Linda, and Victoria Sturtevant. *Hysterical: Women in American Com-
    edy*. University of Texas Press, 2017.

Monagle, Matthew. "Netflix's Nanette and the Importance of Uncomfortable
    Conversations." *Film School Rejects*, 10 Jul. 2018, https://filmschoolrejects.com
    /nanette-netflix/.

Moskowitz, Peter. "The 'Nanette' Problem." *The Outline*, 20 Aug. 2018, https://
    theoutline.com/post/5962/the-nanette-problem-hannah-gadsby-netflix-review.

Nussbaum, Emily. "The Little Tramp: The Raucous Humor of Amy Schumer." *The
    New Yorker*, 11 May 2015.

———. "How Do You Fight an Enemy Who's Just Kidding?" *The New Yorker*, 15
    Jan. 2017.

Nygaard, Taylor. "I'm Cool with It: The Popular Feminism of Inside Amy Schumer."
    Emergent Feminisms: Complicating a Postfeminist Media Culture, edited by
    Jessalynn Keller and Maureen E. Ryan, Routledge, 2018, pp. 57–72.

Onwuachi-Willig, Angela. "What About #UsToo?: The Invisibility of Race in the
    #MeToo Movement." *Yale Law Journal Forum*, vol. 105, 2018, pp. 105–20.

O'Reilly, Bill. *Culture Warrior*. Crown Archetype, 2006.

Paskin, Willa. "The F Word: *Inside Amy Schumer*, the Most Sneakily Feminist Show
    on TV." *Slate*, 1 Apr. 2014.

Pérez, Raúl. "Learning to Make Racism Funny in the 'Color-Blind' Era: Stand-up
    Comedy Students, Performance Strategies, and the (Re)production of Racist
    Jokes in Public." *Discourse and Society*, vol. 24, no. 4, 2013, pp. 478–503.

Petersen, Anne Helen. *Too Fat, Too Slutty, Too Loud: The Rise and Reign of the
    Unruly Woman*. Plume, 2017.

Poniewozik, James. "Trump's Enduring Narrative." *New York Times*, 16 Dec.
    2020, C4.

Prothero, Stephen. *Why Liberals Win (Even When They Lose Elections): How America's Raucous, Nasty, and Mean "Culture Wars" Make for a More Inclusive Nation.* HarperOne, 2016.

Purdie, Susan. *Comedy: The Master of Discourse.* Harvester Wheatsheaf, 1993.

Roberts, Soraya. "Tokens of Appreciation." *The Baffler Magazine,* 8 Oct. 2018, https://thebaffler.com/latest/tokens-of-appreciation-roberts.

Rossing, Jonathan P. "An Ethics of Complicit Criticism for Postmodern Satire." *Studies in American Humor,* vol. 5, no. 1, 2019, pp. 13–30.

———. "Live from D.C., It's Nerd Prom." *Standing Up, Speaking Out: Stand-Up Comedy and the Rhetoric of Social Change,* edited by Matthew R. Meier and Casey R. Schmitt, Routledge, 2017.

Rowe, Kathleen Karlyn. *The Unruly Woman: Gender and the Genres of Laughter.* University of Texas Press, 1995.

Ryzik, Melena. "The Comedy-Destroying, Soul-Affirming Art of Hannah Gadsby." *The New York Times,* 24 Jul. 2018, https://www.nytimes.com/2018/07/24/arts/hannah-gadsby-comedy-nanette.html.

Schumer, Amy. "Information about My 'Formation.'" *Medium,* 27 Oct. 2016.

———. *Inside Amy Schumer.* Comedy Central. Seasons 1–4, 2013–2016.

Sepinwall, Alan. "'Life & Beth' Amy Schumer Goes Home Again." *Rolling Stone,* 8 Mar. 2022.

Shanley, Patrick. "Michelle Wolf Slammed for 'Vile' Sarah Huckabee Sanders Jokes at White House Correspondents' Dinner." *The Hollywood Reporter,* 29 Apr. 2018, https://www.hollywoodreporter.com/news/michelle-wolf-slammed-vile-sarah-huckabee-sanders-jokes-at-white-house-correspondents-dinner-1106776.

Sharf, Zach. "Samantha Bee Gets Honest About Comedy Central Not Wanting Her as 'Daily Show' Host: 'It Was Awful.'" *IndieWire,* 15 May 2019.

Showalter, Dana, Shannon Stevens, and Daniel L. Horvath. *The Misogynistic Backlash Against Woman Strong Films.* Routledge, 2022.

Siapera, Eugenia. "Online Misogyny as Witch Hunt: Primitive Accumulation in the Age of Techno-capitalism." *Gender Hate Online: Understanding the New Anti-Feminism,* edited by Debbie Ging and Eugenia Siapera, Palgrave Macmillan, 2019.

Smith, Taigi. "What Happens When Your Hood Is the Last Stop on the White Flight Express?" *Colonize This! Young Women of Color on Today's Feminism,* edited by Daisy Hernandez and Bushra Rehman, Seal Press, 2002, pp. 50-64.

Sobieraj, Sarah. *Credible Threat: Attacks against Women Online and the Future of Democracy.* Oxford University Press, 2020.

Spencer-Phillips, Mandy. *Gamer Trouble: Feminist Confrontations in Digital Culture.* New York University Press, 2020.

Spigel, Lynn. "Introduction." *Television after TV: Essays on a Medium in Transition,* edited by Lynn Spigel and Jan Olsson, Duke University Press, 2004.

Spigel, Lynn, and Angela McRobbie. *Interrogating Postfeminism: Gender and the Politics of Popular Culture*. Duke University Press, 2007.

St. Felix, Doreen. "'Growing,' Reviewed: What Amy Schumer Won't Expose." *The New Yorker*, 20 Mar. 2019.

The Break with Michelle Wolf. "Strong Female Lead." Episode 1, *Netflix*, 27 May 2018.

———. "Entertainment Explosion." Episode 5, 24 Jun. 2018.

Their, Dave. "2015: The Year Everyone Forgot About Gamergate." *Forbes*, 5 Jan. 2015.

Tomlinson, Barbara. *Feminism and Affect at the Scene of Argument: Beyond the Trope of the Angry Feminist*. Temple University Press, 2010.

Tomsett, Ellie. "Positives and Negatives: Reclaiming the Female Body and Self Deprecation in Stand-up Comedy." *Comedy Studies*, vol. 9, no. 1, 2018, pp. 6–18.

———. "Twenty-first Century Fumerist: Bridget Christie and the Backlash Against Feminist Comedy." *Comedy Studies*, vol. 8, no. 1, 2017, pp. 57–67.

Traister, Rebecca. "Smirking in the Boys' Room." *New York Magazine*, 25 Jan. 2016, http://nymag.com/thecut/2016/01/samantha-bee-full-frontal-c-v-r.html.

"2018 White House Correspondents' Association Dinner." *YouTube*, 29 Apr. 2018, https://www.youtube.com/watch?v=L8IYPnnsYJw.

Vagianos, Alanna. "Watch Amy Schumer Shut Down a Sexist Interviewer Like a Boss." *Huffington Post*, 24 Jul. 2015, https://www.huffpost.com/entry/watch-amy-schumer-shut-down-a-sexist-interviewer-like-a-boss_n_55b2416ee4b0224d8831dbb2.

Vanity Fair [@VanityFair]. "We Talked to All the Titans of Late-Night Television, and Found Out Why Its Better than Ever vnty.fr/1Nzq280." *Twitter*, 14 Sep. 2015, https://twitter.com/VanityFair/status/643459713561141248?ref_src=twsrc%5Etfw%7Ctwcamp%5Etweetembed%7Ctwterm%5E643459713561141248%7Ctwgr%5E9791d7b8b26bee50befac1c69962f805bab9be6f%7Ctwcon%5Es1_&ref_url=https%3A%2F%2Fuproxx.com%2Ftv%2Fsamantha-bee-turned-late-night-ladies-into-centaurs%2F.

West, Lindy. *Shrill: Notes from a Loud Woman*. Hachette, 2017.

White, Sydney. "Mothers and Whores: The Relationship Between Popular Culture and Women in Politics." *Mapping Politics*, vol. 4, 2012, pp. 1–11.

Wright, Megh. "Alt-Right Redditors Have Tanked Amy Schumer's Netflix Ratings for 'The Leather Special.'" *Vulture*, 14 Mar. 2017.

Yancy, George. "Feminism and the Subtext of Whiteness: Black Women's Experiences as a Site of Identity Formation and Contestation of Whiteness." *Western Journal of Black Studies*, vol. 24, no. 3, 156–66.

Yiannopoulos, Milo. "Teenage Boys with Tits: Here's My Problem with Ghostbusters." *Breitbart*, 18 Jul. 2016, http://www.breitbart.com/tech/2016/07/18/milo-reviews-ghostbusters/.

Zimmerman, Amy. "Amy Schumer's Whitewashed Feminism." *The Daily Beast*, 29 Oct. 2016, https://www.thedailybeast.com/amy-schumers-whitewashed -feminism.

Zinoman, Jason. "Amy Schumer Doesn't Care What You Think (That Much)." *New York Times*, 13 Mar. 2019.

INDEX

AMBER DAY is Professor of Media and Performance Studies and Chair of the History, Literature, and the Arts Department at Bryant University. She is author of *Satire and Dissent: Interventions in Contemporary Political Debate* (Indiana University Press, 2011) and editor of *DIY Utopia: Cultural Imagination and the Remaking of the Possible.*

For Indiana University Press

Sabrina Black, Editorial Assistant

Lesley Bolton, Project Manager/Editor

Allison Chaplin, Acquisitions Editor

Anna Garnai, Production Coordinator

Sophia Hebert, Assistant Acquisitions Editor

Samantha Heffner, Marketing and Publicity Manager

Katie Huggins, Production Manager

Dan Pyle, Online Publishing Manager

Pamela Rude, Senior Artist and Book Designer

www.ingramcontent.com/pod-product-compliance
Lightning Source LLC
Chambersburg PA
CBHW030335270326
41926CB00010B/1637